101 Secrets of Gourmet Chefs

Unusual Recipes from Great California Restaurants

EDITED BY JACQUELINE KILLEEN
ILLUSTRATED BY ROY KILLEEN

CONTENTS

TO THOSE WHO HELPED

This book is dedicated to the many chefs who parted with their secret recipes, and particularly to those who gave hours of their time explaining and demonstrating the more difficult dishes; and to the following friends who helped me test the recipes in the home kitchen;

Mr. Tim Blaskovich

Mrs. Alexander Montgomery Haw

Miss Sharon Kessey

Mr. H. M. La Vallee

Mr. Kimun Lee

Mr. David Napier

Miss Sara Raffetto

Mrs. Patrick Robertson

Mrs. Timothy Rose

Mrs. Carol Warren

and with special thanks to Miss Gail Silva, and Miss Sharon Silva, who not only tested an extraordinary number of recipes; but gave invaluable assistance in research and manuscript preparation.

4

The cuisine of any area is a culinary composite of its history, geography and population. Unlike some other parts of the United States, notably New England and the South, California does not have a regional cuisine. Its food is as cosmopolitan as its population.

The California kitchen is as likely to have a Chinese wok as a French whisk and often contains both. Soy sauce, olive oil and French herbs are as basic here as flour and salt. And the average housewife can whip up a veal scallopini or an enchilada with equal ease.

In California we are blessed by an international culinary heritage, rarely found elsewhere, and a unique blending of East and West. We are blessed by an abundance of fresh vegetables, local seafood and excellent wines. We are blessed by a mild and diversified climate which not only attracts settlers from all over the world, but permits them to grow the produce and wines from their native lands. And we are most blessed by our acceptance of new ideas and new experiences; by our eagerness to absorb the culture and cuisine from other lands. No wonder we set a magnificent table!

In this rich and bountiful state, the tradition of good living and good eating goes far back into our history. As early as 1770, the first vineyard was established by the Franciscan fathers at Mission San Diego. The Gold Rush attracted restaurateurs from all countries, eager to share in the quick profits to be made from the free-spending miner who drank champagne like water and would almost sell his stake for a fine soufflé. Later, the Bonanza Kings and the Comstock Lords vied for the services of Europe's great chefs and the contents of France's finest cellars, in an era of opulence that was revived in the golden age of Hollywood. Chinese came to work on the railroads and introduced us to the delights of Oriental food; Italians and Greeks came and built our fishing industry; Frenchmen, Hungarians and Germans brought their cuttings to our vineyards and orchards. All this is part of our tradition.

The tradition of international dining is embodied today in our diversity of fine restaurants. In order to present the outstanding dishes of our composite California cuisine, we have asked the chefs of great restaurants throughout the state for unusual and original recipes, which would be suitable for home preparation. In each case, we have tested the recipe in the home kitchen to make sure that the instructions are clear; that the ingredients are readily available; and that the recipe can be made with ordinary kitchen equipment and average cooking skills. We hope that both the taste and preparation of each dish will be an adventuresome and rewarding experience, for you as it has been for us. J. K.

The first inhabitants of California were Indians. The first European to set foot on California soil was Portugese, Juan Rodriques Cabrillo who headed the Spanish expedition which discovered San Diego Bay in 1542. Ironically, there is almost no Portugese nor Indian tradition in California cuisine.

The state's first settlers, other than the Indians, were the Franciscan fathers who established our missions, and introduced the Spanish-Mediteranean base of California cuisine, by planting vineyards and olive trees. Later the rancheros of Southern California and the Spanish-Mexican families of Monterey continued this tradition. Thus it is also ironic that, although Mexican food is prevalent throughout California to this day, there are surprisingly few authentic Spanish restaurants, other than the Matador, whose recipes we proudly present on the following pages.

Mexican food in California is generally milder than that of Central Mexico, especially in the restaurants we have included in this book. Hot peppers may be added to make the dishes more piquant, to your taste. In preparing Spanish and Mexican food, it is important to use fresh ingredients whenever possible for the best results. This is especially true of tomatoes, as the acid taste of canned tomatoes, (while not objectionable in Italian cooking), becomes quite apparent in Spanish food. Mexican food, to our taste, is best accompanied by beer; Spanish food, by wine.

GAZPACHO

Serves Ten
1 tablespoon minced parsley
1 teaspoon minced fresh tarragon
1 green pepper, chopped
1 cucumber, peeled and seeded
8 scallions or 2 medium sized
  onions, chopped
2 pounds fresh tomatoes,
  peeled and seeded
2 tablespoons tomato paste
1/4 cup olive oil
1/2 teaspoon salt, or to taste
1 teaspoon lemon juice
  (or 1 tablespoon white vinegar)
1 12-ounce can mixed vegetable juice
3 cups clear fat-free chicken broth
minced green pepper and
  cucumber for garnish

Be sure to seed tomatoes and cucumbers thoroughly. Crush minced parsley and tarragon together until pastelike and add to green pepper and cucumber. Put in blender and run at low speed until pureed. Add scallions or onions and finally tomatoes. Blend until well pureed. Add olive oil gradually while blender is in motion, then salt, lemon juice, vegetable juice, and, if a richer red color is desired, two tablespoons tomato paste. Blend with chicken stock. Chill for several hours, the longer the better. Serve with an ice cube in each dish, passing green pepper and cucumber garnish.

PAELLA A LA VALENCIANA

Serves Six to Eight
1 small chicken, cut up
2 large white onions, chopped
3 green onions chopped
1 shallot, chopped finely
olive oil
1/2 pound large shrimps
2 rock lobster tails, thickly sliced
1 bay leaf
salt and pepper
2 cups uncooked rice
1/4 pound green peas
1/4 pound string beans
1 large Spanish sausage (Chorizo) sliced
1 thick slice of ham, cut in squares
2 ripe tomatoes, peeled and diced
1 pinch saffron
chicken stock
1 can (7 ounce) red pimientos
black olives
green olives
1 dozen fresh clams in the shell,
  scrubbed well

In a paella pan (or large skillet which can be placed in the oven), sauté the chickens with onions and shallots until golden brown. At the same time, in another pan, simmer the lobster, shrimp, bay leaf in 3/4 cup olive oil, seasoned with salt and pepper, for 20 minutes. Drain seafood and combine with cooked chicken in larger pan. Add rice, peas, beans, sausage, ham and tomato. Season with salt, pepper and saffron. Cover pan with stock and cook, covered, over medium fire until rice is *almost* done. (It is important not to overcook rice which should still be very moist at this point.) Decorate with pimientos, black and green olives and clams. Bake at 350° for nine minutes, or until the clams have opened.

LANGOSTA A LA BILBAINA

Serves Four
2 pounds lobster tails
4 tablespoons butter
1 shallot, minced
1/2 pound sliced fresh mushrooms
1 bell pepper, chopped
1 4-ounce jar pimientos
1/2 teaspoon English dry mustard
1 tablespoon worcestershire sauce
1/2 cup Spanish dry sherry

Sauce
1 egg yolk, room temperature
3 tablespoons melted butter
1 cup cream
1 teaspoon lemon juice
1/4 cup parmesan cheese
1/2 teaspoon salt

First make the sauce. In a double boiler, over very low heat, stir the egg yolk until it thickens. Remove from fire and slowly add melted butter, drop by drop, stirring constantly until thick and creamy. Add cream, then lemon juice, salt and cheese; stir over low heat until well blended. Remove from heat and reserve.

To prepare the dish, remove the lobster meat from the shells and cut into cubes. Saute the shallots in butter a few minutes; then add the green peppers and mushrooms and cook a few minutes longer. Add the lobster and cook for 5 minutes over a slow fire. Add remaining ingredients and mix well. Remove from heat and slowly blend in the cream sauce. Place under a broiler for three minutes and serve with rice.

ESCALOPE DE TERNERA VASCA

Serves Six
2½ pounds veal loin, sliced thin
1 large green pepper
18 slices pimiento
12 black olives, sliced
1/2 pound mushrooms
3 tomatoes
2 cloves garlic
1 pinch minced chives
salt and pepper
1 cup vegetable oil
1/2 cup olive oil
pinch oregano
1 cup Amontillado (medium sherry)

Pound veal slices, dredge in flour and sauté in olive-vegetable oil mixture. Add chives, green pepper, garlic, oregano, salt and pepper, and simmer for 15 minutes. Add sherry, tomatoes and mushrooms; simmer another 10 minutes. Add olives and pimientos and cook a few minutes longer. Serve with white rice or saffron rice.

PORK WITH GREEN CHILE

Serves Four to Six
2 pounds pork loin
2 garlic cloves, minced
1½ cups cooking oil
1 large onion, chopped
1½ cups whole, peeled tomatoes
2 cups tomatillo (3 small cans)
6 large, long green mild chiles

Jerry Torres, owner of El Poche, recommends fresh Anaheim chiles if available. If fresh chiles are used, peel by first blanching in hot oil, or blistering skin on open gas flame. Remove seeds, veins and stems; and cut into strips, lengthwise. Canned Ortega chiles may be substituted, but may lack "authority," which can be attained by adding some minced Ortega hot chiles. Usually the fresh chiles will be hot enough. To prepare the dish, cut the pork into 3/4 inch cubes, leaving a little fat on some of the pieces. Add minced garlic to oil; heat; then brown the pork in the hot oil. Add onion, tomatoes and chili strips. Mix well and cook until pork is well done but not too dry. Add salt and pepper to taste, tomatillo and simmer for 15 minutes.

GREEN CHILE AND GUACAMOLE SALAD

Serves Six
6 medium mild green chiles
6 cups guacamole (see below)
1 cup water chestnuts, chopped in chunks
1 pound cooked shrimp, chopped in chunks
1/2 pound Swiss cheese, grated
lettuce leaves
oil and vinegar salad dressing

Again Jerry Torres recommends fresh Anaheim chiles. If used, peel according to method in Pork and Chile, but leave on the stem. Slit one side to remove the seeds and veins. Make your favorite guacamole recipe (or use Los Gallos'—see index), and add the chopped chestnuts and shrimp. Stuff the peppers and place, slit side down, over lettuce on individual salad plates. Pour salad dressing over the chile and garnish lightly with grated cheese.

GUACAMOLE SALAD

Serves Four
4 ripe avocados
juice of 1 lemon
1 small can Spanish green tomatoes
2 mild green (Ortega) chiles
2 green onions, chopped
1 garlic clove, mashed (optional)
salt and pepper
lettuce
grated Monterey Jack cheese
tomato wedges
oil and vinegar

Los Gallos is noted for its very mild and subtle
guacamole, which can be served either in the salad or
as a dip with fritos. To make the guacamole, peel,
seed and mash the avocados. Add lemon juice, tomatoes, chiles, onions, garlic and salt and pepper to
taste. Run through blender and correct seasoning.
(Los Gallos recommends no garlic and only two
chiles, but suggests that some cooks would want to
add more chiles to taste.) To make the salad, sprinkle
an oil and vinegar dressing over lettuce on individual
plates. Top with a ladle of guacamole and garnish
with Monterey Jack (or any mild white cheese) and
tomato wedges.

CARNE ASADA

Serves Four
New York cut or top sirloin steak
2 tablespoons butter
2 medium onions, sliced
2 garlic cloves, mashed
4 *mild* green chiles, sliced
1½ cups salsa (see below)
3 tablespoons *juice only* canned
   hot green peppers
corn tortillas

Sauté onions, garlic and mild green chiles in butter until the onions are clear. Add salsa and the juice only from the hot green peppers. (This recipe is relatively mild and if you like hot food, add more of the hot pepper juice.) Cook mixture until it comes to a boil and pour over the broiled steak. Serve with heated corn tortillas, in which your guests can roll pieces of the meat and sauce.

Salsa a la Los Gallos
Makes 1½ cups
3 or 4 fresh tomatoes, peeled and chopped fine
1 hot, fresh yellow pepper, chopped
3 green onions, chopped fine
1 small garlic clove (optional)
salt to taste.

Mix all ingredients together, adding more hot yellow pepper for hotness if desired. (Los Gallos' salsa is medium hot.) This recipe can be served in a side dish as a condiment for all Mexican dishes and is an excellent accompaniment for pork, chicken and shrimp as well. It can be refrigerated for several weeks.

THE FAR EAST

The Chinese came to California in the 1840's to dig for gold in the Mother Lode, where many cooked for the miners rather than pan for gold. But the gigantic immigration was in the 1860's, when 15,000 Chinese came to California for the construction of the Central Pacific Railroad. When this job was completed, most moved to the cities and many started restaurants. By 1880, there were 74,000 Chinese in California and their food has had a major impact on the California cuisine.

Until recently, most Chinese came here from the province of Canton and the extensive culinary tradition of the other provinces was virtually unknown to Californians, until the Communist take over drove many residents of Shanghai and Peking to this country. Some started restaurants and the intricate Mandarin cuisine was introduced to California.

The Japanese did not arrive in California in large numbers until the 1890's, and until recent years there were not many Japanese restaurants. Yamato, whose recipes we present here, was the first of significance.

The secret of cooking Chinese and Japanese food is quickness. Everything should be fresh, cooked briefly over high heat, and served immediately. For this a Chinese wok pot is far more effective than a skillet. Oriental food should always be accompanied by white rice and tea.

MANCHURIAN BEEF

Serves Four
1 pound beef sirloin
1/4 cup light Chinese soy sauce
1/4 cup dry sherry
1 garlic clove, finely chopped
1 ginger tube, 3/4 inch in diameter,
  thinly sliced
1/2 tablespoon sugar
1/4 tablespoon salt
1—1½ tablespoons cornstarch
1/2 pound sliced mushrooms
peanut oil

Mix cornstarch with several tablespoons of the soy sauce until smooth. Add remaining soy sauce, wine, sugar and sliced ginger. Cut beef into 1/2 inch cubes, mix into sauce and marinate for about one hour. In a wok or skillet, heat several tablespoons of peanut oil to which salt and one slice of ginger has been added until very hot. Strain marinade from the beef, saving the sauce, and brown beef on both sides until medium or rare as desired. Add garlic and mushrooms and stir a few minutes over hot fire. Add marinade sauce and thicken, if necessary, with a little cornstarch blended with water; stir and serve.

EMPRESS LOBSTER

Serves Four to Eight
6 lobster tails; 6 ounces each
1 bamboo shoot, sliced diagonally
6 Chinese mushrooms
12 water chestnuts, cut in half
1 egg white
cornstarch
light Chinese soy sauce
sugar
peanut oil

Soak mushrooms in water until soft, then cut in half. Shell lobster and cut into one inch cubes. Mix egg white and a teaspoon corn starch until well blended. Then mix lobster cubes into eggwhite until well coated and marinate about ten minutes. Sauté lobster in a little peanut oil in a hot skillet or wok very quickly. Sprinkle with salt; add mushrooms, water chestnuts and bamboo shoots; cover pan; bring to boil; and allow to boil for five minutes. When the lobster is cooked, pour in a thickening made from 1 teaspoon cornstarch (dissolved in a little water), 2 tablespoons soy sauce, 1/2 teaspoon sugar and 1/4 cup water. (Note: Serves four as a main course, eight as a first course or banquet course.)

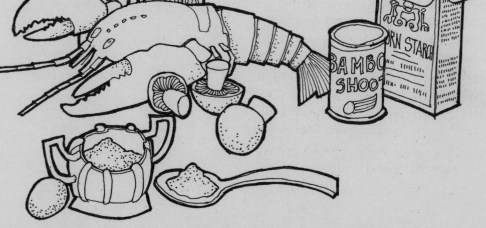

GARDEN ORIENTALE LEE ON
Green and White Vegetables

Serves Four
2 pounds heart of mustard greens
2 pounds heart of chinese cabbage
2 cups chicken stock
1/2 cup cream
1 teaspoon ham oil or bacon fat
1 dash sesame seed oil
cornstarch
finely chopped Virginia ham

Chef Lee On is noted for his proficiency in both the Chinese and French cuisines. Though this is a Chinese dish, it has a decidedly French accent. Separate vegetables from stalks and slice into strips of uniform size. (Broccoli and bean sprouts can be substituted as vegetables.) Boil vegetables in chicken stock until tender. Drain, reserving stock, and arrange on platter. In a saucepan combine 1/2 cup of the chicken-vegetable stock with ham oil, sesame seed oil and salt and stir over low heat for several minutes. Add cream and thicken with a little cornstarch blended with a little cream. Serve sauce over the vegetables and garnish with chopped ham. Note: Be sure to use sesame *seed* oil, not sesame cooking oil.

STEAMED WHOLE FISH A LA LEE ON

Serves Four
2½–3½ pound whole rock cod, cleaned
1 ounce dehydrated black mushrooms
1 ounce shredded bamboo shoot
1 ounce shredded green onion
1 tablespoon chopped fresh ginger
1 ounce shredded Virginia ham
soy sauce
1 pinch salt
1 pinch white pepper
1 pinch sugar
1 tablespoon oyster sauce
corn starch
2 tablespoon peanut oil

If possible, have a Chinese butcher clean and prepare the rock cod for you, leaving the head, bones and tail remaining in typical Chinese style. Soak the mushrooms in water until soft and then shred. Shred other vegetables into very thin strips about two inches long. (Be sure to slice bamboo shoots diagonally before shredding or they will not be tender). Place the whole fish on an oven proof platter, which will fit into one of your larger cooking pots. Dissolve 1 tablespoon cornstarch in 2 tablespoons soy sauce; add ginger, salt, pepper, sugar, oyster sauce and peanut oil; and pour sauce over fish. Then sprinkle shredded mushrooms, bamboo shoots, and ham over fish. Place platter on a rack in a pan of boiling water, so that water does not boil into platter; cover and steam 10 minutes per pound or until fish is flaky and tender.

CHEF MEE WAH JANG'S CASHEW CHICKEN

Serves Four to Six

1½ pounds chicken breasts
cornstarch
3/4 cup unsalted cashew nuts
1/2 teaspoon salt
1/2 cup chicken stock
3/4 cup sliced bamboo shoots, cut
    in 1/4 x 1½-inch pieces
1 cup snow peas, stringed
1/2 teaspoon sugar
peanut oil
soy sauce
1/2 teaspoon MSG
1 garlic clove, mashed (optional)
pepper to taste

Bone and skin chicken. Slice meat wafer-thin and cut in 1½-inch squares. Marinate chicken for 15 minutes in a mixture of one tablespoon peanut oil, one tablespoon soy sauce and one teaspoon cornstarch. Sauté nut meats in one tablespoon peanut oil until nuts are slightly brown. In another extremely hot frying pan or wok, place three tablespoons peanut oil, salt, and garlic, if used. Add chicken and sauté on high fire until chicken meat turns white. Add stock, mushrooms, bamboo shoots, and snow peas. Cover and cook for 1 minute before adding pepper, MSG, sugar, two teaspoons soy sauce, and two teaspoons cornstarch mixed with two teaspoons water. Stir gently until sauce thickens. Pour in nut meat, mix slightly, and serve piping hot.

22

CHEF MEE WAH JANG'S SWEET AND SOUR PORK

Serves Six to Eight

1 pound pork butt
1/4 teaspoon MSG
cornstarch
1 green pepper, seeded and cut in
   1-inch chunks
1 large tomato, cut in wedges
1/4 cup white vinegar
1/2 cup tomato catsup
1/4 cup water, or pineapple juice
1 egg
1 teaspoon soy sauce
salt
cracker meal
3/4 cup pineapple chunks
6 tablespoons sugar, or more to taste
1 teaspoon worcestershire sauce
2 dashes tabasco sauce
vegetable or peanut oil

Dice pork in 1/2 inch squares. Prepare mixture of egg, 1/4 teaspoon salt, MSG, soy sauce, and two tablespoons cornstarch. Dip pork squares in egg mixture, then roll in cracker meal. Let stand until coating dries, (about 30 minutes) before cooking meat. Deep fry (350°) in vegetable or peanut oil for 10 minutes until meat is thoroughly cooked. Prepare sweet and sour sauce by combining vinegar, catsup, water, sugar, worcestershire sauce, a pinch of salt, and tabasco sauce in a small sauce pan. Bring to a slow boil and simmer for 30 seconds. In a large frying pan or wok, place the sweet and sour sauce. Bring to a boil before adding the pieces of green pepper and cook for 30 seconds. Add one tablespoon of cornstarch mixed with two tablespoons of water, then the tomato wedges, pineapple chunks, and pork cubes. Stir and cook quickly for 15 seconds until the sauce is evenly mixed.

FUJI BEEF

Serves Six
3/4 pound flank steak
4 black dehydrated mushrooms
2 celery branches
8 green onions
24 Chinese pea-pods
8 ounces bamboo shoots
chicken stock
1/2 teaspoon MSG
2 tablespoons soy sauce
1 ounce sherry
2 teaspoon corn starch
safflower oil

Slice beef and vegetables diagonally into long thin strips. Mix beef with salt, MSG, soy sauce, sherry, corn starch and enough safflower oil to moisten the mixture; and marinate for at least 15 minutes. In a heavy skillet or wok heat enough safflower oil to just cover beef. When oil is hot, add beef and cook very quickly (40 to 60 seconds) until beef is just browned. Remove beef and drain. In another frying pan or wok, sauté vegetables in safflower oil quickly, stirring constantly. Cover with chicken stock and bring to boil. Add soy sauce and MSG to taste and thicken with cornstarch blended with water. At the last minute, add the precooked beef. Serve covered with deep fried rice noodles.

PEACH BLOSSOM DUCK

Serves Six as Banquet Course
3 whole duck breasts (see note below)
salt and pepper
Chinese hung ley (five spices)
1/8 cup light soy sauce
1/8 cup brandy
star anise
peanut or sesame oil
fine waterchestnut flour
2 tablespoons melted butter
MSG
6 peach halves
Indian chutney

To serve this dish properly, as at Trader Vic's, only the breasts should be used. We found in testing, however, that by adding the drumstick and thigh, cooked and seasoned in the same manner as the breast, there is sufficient meat to serve the dish as a main course. The hung ley, waterchestnut flour and star anise can be purchased at most Chinese grocery stores. To prepare the dish, cut the breasts (and the drumstick and thigh if you are going to use them) out of the duck with poultry shears, leaving on the fat and skin. Sprinkle, inside and out, with salt, pepper and hung ley. Marinate duck overnight in soy sauce and brandy (increase portions for leg and thigh). To cook, deep fry the duck in oil until golden brown and drain. Next, simmer in water, to which star anise has been added for one hour or until tender. Remove from stock; drain; sprinkle very lightly with sifted waterchestnut flour. Cook in pressure cooker for 3 to 5 minutes or bake in hot oven for about 10 minutes or until flour is transparent. Cool and trim out the breast bone only and divide each breast into two portions. When ready to serve, deep fry in oil for 5 minutes; brush with melted butter; sprinkle with a mixture of 2 parts MSG and 1 part hung ley. (The meat should be moist and the skin should be crisp.) At Trader Vic's, the duck is served with a broiled peach half topped with chutney and deep fried shredded bok choy (Chinese greens).

HOT AND SOUR SOUP

Serves Four
4 cups chicken stock or broth
2 pieces fresh white tofu
  (Chinese bean curd) cubed
6—8 chopped small shrimp
1 teaspoon chopped pork, raw
1 teaspoon chopped chicken, raw
1 teaspoon chopped chicken liver (raw)
sliced bamboo shoots (optional)
two beaten eggs
salt
1/2 teaspoon white pepper
1 tablespoon red wine vinegar
dash soy sauce

This is a typical soup of Northern China. Bring chicken broth to boil and toss in shrimp, chopped meats, vegetables and tofu. Simmer a few minutes until ingredients are cooked and then add beaten eggs. Simmer a few minutes more and add salt and white pepper to taste, vinegar and soy sauce.

San Francisco

GRILLED AND STEAMED CHIAO-TZU
(CHINESE RAVIOLIS)

2 cups white wheat all-purpose flour
1 cup water
1/3 cup cooked prawns, chopped
1/3 cup lean uncooked pork
1/3 cup fresh raw chinese cabbage
grated fresh ginger root
finely chopped green onion tops
chopped coriander greens (Chinese parsley)
2 tablespoons sesame oil
soy sauce
1 tablespoon clear chicken stock

Make a paste of flour and water and meld by hand until very smooth, adding enough water to make it firm but not hard. Cover with a dusting of flour and an inverted bowl and leave at room temperature for at least four hours. For the filling, chop prawns, pork and cabbage very fine and mix with grated ginger, green onion tops and coriander greens to taste. Add oil and soy sauce and check seasoning. Place in refrigerator for at least one hour before using.

Before stuffing raviolis add about one tablespoon chicken stock to filling so that the mixture is moist but not soggy. Then tear off small pieces of the dough, about the size of a large marble. Roll out very thin on floured board to the shape of a circle and press together with the dry side to form a half-moon shaped ravioli, but put the seam upright, crimped into a fluted center line with the bottom flat. These may be placed in refrigerator until ready to cook.

To cook the Chiao Tzu, heat an iron frying pan very hot, brush the bottom with a fine film of sesame oil, and place the ravioli flat side down on the surface. Immediately add one cup of cold water to the pan and cover tightly. The water will evaporate in about six minutes and the bottoms of the Chiao Tzu will be brown and crisp and the sides moistly steamed. At the Mandarin these are served with small bottles of white vinegar and hot pepper oil for dunking.

SHRIMP SCHEZWAN

Serves Four as Banquet Course
1 pound shrimp or prawns, uncooked
2 garlic cloves, pressed
1 tablespoon fresh ginger root, chopped
2–4 small red chile peppers, crushed
1½ tablespoons soy sauce
2 tablespoons catsup
1 bunch green onions, chopped
pinch of salt
2 teaspoons sugar
dash sesame seed oil
cooking oil

This dish is traditionally served *extremely* hot, but can be tempered to taste by reducing the amount of red peppers. Cover iron skillet or wok lightly with cooking oil and heat until the oil is very hot. Quickly sauté the shrimp over very hot flame until the shrimp turns white. Add all other ingredients except the onions with just enough water or stock to keep from burning. Cook, stirring, until the shrimp are coated and the water has evaporated. Add the onions and cook a few minutes longer. Serve immediately.

CUCUMBER SALAD (SUNOMONO)

Serves Four
1 pound cucumbers, peeled
1 cup cider vinegar
3/4 cup sugar
salt
1 teaspoon MSG
cooked crab, shrimp and/or
    abalone (garnish)
sliced tomatoes (garnish)

Cut cucumbers in half; slice lengthwise; sprinkle lightly with salt; mix well and allow to marinate for awhile. Then squeeze dry with your hand; rinse and drain well. Combine vinegar, sugar and MSG; pour enough of this dressing over the cucumbers to coat them and allow to marinate for awhile. Squeeze dry again and chill. When ready to serve, add the remainder of the dressing to the cucumbers; toss gently and place the cucumbers in individual bowls. Garnish with cooked seafood and sliced tomatoes.

BUTTER-YAKI

Serves Four

2½ cups sliced mushrooms
1 pound green onions, cut
   in 1½ inch pieces
1/4 pound butter, melted
1½ pounds top sirloin of beef
1 tablespoon Japanese soy sauce
1½ tablespoons lemon juice
1/8 teaspoon Japanese wasabi
(horseradish or dry English mustard
   may be substituted for wasabi)

Make a dipping sauce by combining soy sauce, lemon juice and wasabi to taste for hotness. Slice beef into strips as thin as a slice of bacon. Sauté mushrooms and onions in butter until tender. Add the beef and cook to desired degree. Serve with sauce poured into individual bowls for dipping the butter-yaki.

TETSU-YAKI

Serves Four

2½ pounds halibut (or sea bass
    or salmon or chicken)
1/3 cup Japanese soy sauce
2/3 cup sweet sherry
1/3 cup sugar
1½ tablespoons salt
1/3 cup sake (or dry sherry)
1/2 pound green onions, cut
    in 2-inch pieces
2 teaspoons salad oil
1/2 lemon

Bone fish and cut into pieces approximately 4 inches square and 3/4 inch thick. Salt generously and let stand for three hours in refrigerator. Combine soy sauce, sherry, sugar and MSG; marinate fish in this mixture in refrigerator for at least 3 hours (or overnight). When ready to serve, remove the fish from the marinade (keeping the marinade), and place on a bed of green onions in an ovenproof serving dish. Sprinkle the oil over the fish to keep it from drying and broil in a hot oven approximately four minutes per side. Pour the marinade over the fish and serve with lemon wedges.

31

The first Italians came to California with the Spanish missionaries. More came for the Gold Rush in the 1850's, but soon gravitated from the inland gold fields to the coastal ports and fertile wine-growing valleys of California. The first Italians were predominately from the Southern Italian seacoast, many from Sicily, and they utilized their skills to develop California's fishing industry, which by 1890 ranked sixth in the nation. Catching the fish led naturally to opening seafood restaurants, where fish was of course prepared in the Italian style. Thus the California cuisine acquired a strong Italian accent.

The first Italians who came here and the large immigration of the early 1900's were mostly from Southern Italy and they brought with them the highly seasoned, garlic-and-olive-oil cuisine of that area. Most Californians were not aware of the subtle cuisine of Northern Italy until the post World War II period when, for example, cannelloni was first introduced in California restaurants. Today, some of our finest Italian chefs are from Tuscany or Bologna.

The Italian recipes which follow include both the Northern and Southern methods of cooking. Southern food is usually cooked in olive oil and heavily spiced; northern food in butter and lightly seasoned; and the distinction is important to the final result. When cooking Italian dishes, always use fresh garlic, fresh herbs whenever available, and fresh vegetables. For veal recipes, buy your meat from an Italian butcher who can cut and pound it properly; and insist on the whitest meat available. Sautéed veal must be young and tender and the whiter the meat, the younger the calf.

ANTHONY'S CIOPPINO

Serves Four
1 1½-pound lobster
2 pounds mixed raw fish in chunks
  (sculpin, snapper, rock cod, sea bass, etc.)
6—8 raw shrimp in shells
1 pound raw clams in shells
Catherine Ghio's Tomato Sauce

The secret of a good cioppino, or Italian fisherman's stew, is a variety of fish. So don't be afraid to mix as many types of fish as you wish. Ask your butcher or fish dealer to get a live lobster for you and to cut it up live into chunks, shells and all, for cioppino. Make Catherine Ghio's Tomato Sauce from recipe on the following page with the following changes: (1) Double all the ingredients, except the garlic and oil, which should only be increased slightly. (2) Add two small cans of tomato paste and do not add the tomato sauce. Add the chunks of raw lobster to the sauce, with shells, and simmer for 20 minutes. Next add the raw mixed fish and simmer for 15 minutes. Finally add the shrimp and clams and cook for five minutes. While cooking keep pot covered and shake periodically so that the fish will not stick to the bottom. Do not stir as this will cause the fish to break. Add water if sauce begins to thicken. Serve in bowls with hot french bread to dunk into the sauce.

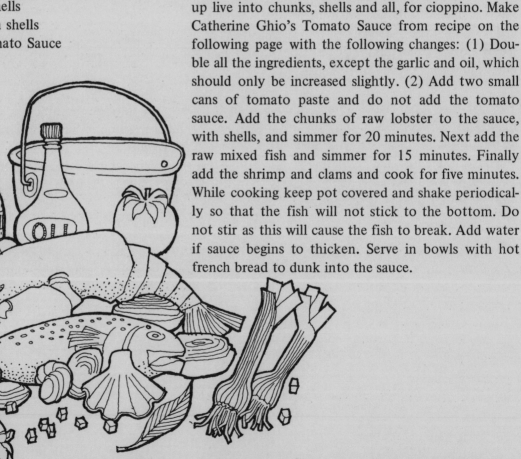

ANTHONY'S BAKED FISH

Serves Four
4 fish steaks (or 1 whole fish)
4 small potatoes
Catherine Ghio's Tomato Sauce

Catherine Ghio, founder of Anthony's famed fish grottos, suggests the following method as a delicious, yet simple and healthful, way of preparing almost any fish—salmon, halibut, sea bass, sole, etc. Make tomato sauce as described below. Pour half of sauce into bottom of an ungreased, flat baking dish. Place fish in dish and cover with remainder of sauce. Arrange peeled and sliced potatoes around the fish. Bake 45 minutes in oven that has been preheated to 400°, turning down to 350° about half way through the cooking time. Be very careful that the sauce does not dry out. If it starts to evaporate, add water.

Catherine Ghio's Tomato Sauce
4 tablespoon polyunsaturated oil
  (or olive oil)
1 medium onion, coarsely chopped
2 ounces dry white wine
4 garlic cloves, chopped very fine
5 sprigs of parsley, chopped
1 11-ounce can pear tomatoes
1/4 teaspoon black pepper
salt to taste
1 pinch thyme
1 8-ounce can Spanish tomato sauce

Sauté onions in oil until golden brown. Add garlic and parsley and cook about 5 minutes being careful not to let the garlic burn. Add wine and stir. Drain tomatoes, but save the juice, and shop tomatoes. Add tomatoes, tomato juice, tomato sauce and seasonings to onions and garlic and simmer about 15 minutes. When cooked add 1 cup hot water.

CANNELLONI

Tomato Sauce (Six Cups)
1/2 large onion, chopped fine
1 cup chicken broth
1/4 teaspoon oregano
1/4 teaspoon fresh basil
1 small clove garlic, chopped fine
1 #2½ can solid-pack tomatoes
1/4 cup olive oil
pinch of thyme
salt and pepper

Heat the olive oil in a saucepan. Add onion and garlic. Cook for 3 or 4 minutes, stirring constantly until the onion begins to brown. Add the chopped solid packed tomatoes, thyme, salt, and pepper and cook the sauce for ten minutes. Then add the chicken broth and continue to cook slowly over a low flame for about forty minutes until it becomes thick. Add the basil and season to taste.

Filling (For Approximately 24 Cannelloni)
1 onion, chopped fine
1 clove garlic, chopped fine
1/2 pound boned veal
1/2 pound boned chicken
1/2 cup half-and-half
3 egg yolks
1/2 cup butter
1 pound ricotta or small curd
    cottage cheese
1 sprig rosemary
salt and pepper
1/2 cup parmesan cheese
2 pounds teleme cheese
1 dash nutmeg

Sauté the onion and garlic in butter until they are browned. Add the chicken, veal, rosemary, salt, and pepper. Stir and cook until done. Put the mixture through a meat grinder. Blend with the ricotta, egg yolks, nutmeg, parmesan cheese and half-and-half. Season to taste, Put a little of this filling on each pancake and roll each one to form a tube. Pour 1/3 of 1 inch tomato sauce in a shallow baking dish. Arrange the cannelloni side by side. Bake in oven (350°) for ten minutes. Then on top of each one, add a strip of teleme cheese. Return to oven until the cheese is melted. Serve immediately, with remaining sauce.

Pancake Batter
3 eggs
1 teaspoon salt
butter
1 cup flour
2½ cups milk

Beat the egg, add salt, milk, flour, and two tablespoons of butter. Beat well, then strain. Melt a little butter in a small heavy skillet, 5½ inches in diameter. Pour enough batter into the pan to cover the bottom (about two tablespoons or a one-ounce ladle). Cook over medium heat until pancake is delicately golden brown. Turn with a spatula and brown the other side.

STUFFED TOMATOES DE MEDICI

Serves Four
2 tomatoes
1/2 onion, chopped
1/2 pound mushrooms, chopped
1/2 cup fine white breadcrumbs
3 tablespoons parmesan cheese
2 tablespoons chopped parsley
pinch oregano
1 egg
4 mushroom caps
salt and pepper
butter

Cut tomatoes in half and scoop out soft part. Sauté onion in butter until soft; then add chopped mushrooms and sauté until soft. Remove from fire and add bread crumbs, cheese, parsley, seasonings and egg. Mix well and stuff tomato halves with mixture. Top each portion with a mushroom cap and bake in moderate oven (350°) for about 15 minutes or until well heated throughout.

SCALLOPPINE OF VEAL A LA PAOLO

Serves Four
12 thin slices veal loin, pounded flat
salt, pepper and flour
butter
1/4 cup dry sauterne wine
1 pound sliced mushrooms
1/2 cup brown sauce (see index)
12 thin slices eggplant, peeled
1 tablespoon shallots
chopped parsley

In separate pans, sauté mushrooms in butter and floured egg plant in butter and oil. Season veal with salt and pepper; dust it lightly with flour. Melt 1/2 pound butter in large skillet until bubbling; then add the veal slices and brown on both sides. Pour off excess butter; add wine and shallots; ignite and simmer for 3 minutes after flame burns out. Blend in brown sauce. To serve, place a bed of the sauteed mushrooms on the serving dish and alternate veal and egg plant slices on top. Add two tablespoons butter to the sauce in skillet and swirl to melt the butter; then pour the sauce over the veal and egg plant slices. Serve immediately.

SCAMPI AND PROSCIUTTO

12 medium size shrimp
12 slices proscuitto (ham)
olive oil
2 cloves garlic, pressed
oregano
4 tablespoons white wine
1 tablespoon lemon juice
2 tablespoons butter
1 teaspoon flour
MSG
chopped parsley

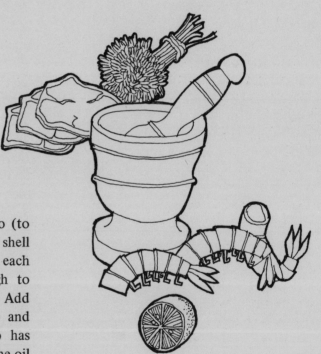

With a mortar and pestle crush a little oregano (to taste) into several tablespoons olive oil. Remove shell from shrimp, devein, but leave on tail. Wrap each shrimp with one slice proscuitto, just enough to cover. Heat olive oil and garlic in heavy pan. Add shrimp. Brush oil and oregano on the shrimp and place under the broiler until the proscuitto has browned, approximately 2 minutes. Drain off the oil from the pan. Add the white wine and simmer a little to reduce the wine; then add lemon juice and butter. In another pan heat three tablespoons oil. Bring to boiling point and blend in one teaspoon flour. Add to shrimp. Sprinkle with MSG and parsley and serve.

VEAL MATTEO

Serves Four
8 2-ounce veal scallops
salt
pepper
MSG
flour
2 eggs
olive oil
romano cheese
parmesan cheese
8 slices eggplant, 1/4-inch thick
8 slices mozarella cheese
marinara sauce (see below)

Marinara Sauce
2 branches celery, chopped fine
1/2 onion, chopped fine
1 green pepper, chopped fine
1 clove garlic, chopped fine
1 teaspoon salt
1 teaspoon oregano
1 teaspoon basil
1 jigger marsala wine
1 tablespoon worcestershire sauce
2 16-ounce cans tomatoes, coarsely
  chopped with liquid
olive oil

Remove gristle from veal and pound until almost paper thin. Season veal with salt, pepper, and MSG. Dust with flour and dip in one beaten egg. Brown both sides in olive oil very quickly over high flame. Meanwhile, dredge eggplant in flour and salt and dip in egg. Fry both sides until golden brown. Pour a layer of marinara sauce in a fireproof baking dish. Add a layer of veal and sprinkle with romano, parmesan, MSG, and freshly-ground black pepper. Add another layer of marinara sauce. Sprinkle again with romano, parmesan, and MSG. On top of this place slices of fried eggplant. Sprinkle again with parmesan, romano, and MSG. Top with marinara sauce. Cover with eight slices of mozarella cheese and top with grated romano. Put under broiler until cheese melts and browns.

Sauté all of the ingredients, except the tomatoes, in the olive oil. Add tomatoes and simmer for 30 minutes.

LUPO'S COO-COO CLAMS

For Each Serving
6 medium-size clams
8 tablespoons olive oil
3 tablespoons red wine vinegar
1 crushed garlic clove
1/4 teaspoon chopped parsley
1/4 teaspoon oregano
1/4 teaspoon basil
1 pinch dried red chile pepper
1 pinch salt
1 pinch pepper
french bread

This dish was created by Lupo in the 1950's. The secret is to use medium size clams, about two inches long. Wash clams thoroughly and place unopened shells in individual baking dishes for each serving. Mix together oil, vinegar and seasonings and mix around clam shells. Bake uncovered at 450°for approximately 25 minutes, or for 15 to 20 minutes after the clams have opened. Serve with french bread for dunking the sauce. If you wish to bake the clams in one large casserole, rather than in the individual dishes, do not increase the sauce proportionately. Instead, add 1 tablespoon oil, 1 teaspoon vinegar, a pinch of the herbs, and salt and pepper to taste for each half-dozen additional clams.

MIRO'S SPECIAL

Serves Four
12 thin slices veal loin
12 thin slices prosciutto
12 slices mozarella cheese
pepper
flour
egg
breadcrumbs
corn oil

This is the creation of Ramiro Tomarich, owner of Old Trieste. Pound veal until very thin. On each veal slice, place a slice of prosciutto, then a slice of mozarella. Season with pepper, fold in half; dust with flour; dip in egg and press into breadcrumbs. Sauté in a preheated hot skillet in corn oil until golden brown (several minutes on each side). Place in baking dish and bake at 375° for about ten minutes. Serve immediately with supreme sauce. (You may fix the slices ahead of time, but do not bread until the last minute!)

SUPREME SAUCE A LA OLD TRIESTE

Two Cups
6 tablespoons butter
4 tablespoons flour
2 cups milk
1 tablespoon sherry
1/2 pound mushrooms

Chop mushrooms finely and sauté in 1 tablespoon butter. Melt remaining 4 tablespoons butter in another pan over low heat. Blend in flour, add milk and stir constantly until sauce has thickened. Add sauteed mushrooms and sherry. This sauce may be used on other dishes such as cannelloni.

STRACCIATELLA ALLA ROMANA

Serves Four
4 cups chicken broth
2 eggs
1 teaspoon chopped fresh parsley
2 tablespoons grated parmesan cheese
small pinch nutmeg

Beat together eggs, cheese and spices. Bring consomme to the boiling point and add the cheese mixture. Boil for one minute, breaking up the egg and cheese mixture with a fork. Serve immediately.

LAMB DE MEDICI

For Two Servings
1 rack of lamb (see below)
4 thin slices prosciutto ham
fontina cheese
butter
1/2 cup marsala wine
1 cup chicken consomme
1 tablespoon brandy
salt and pepper

Have your butcher prepare the lamb by removing the bones and fat, leaving only the eye of the rack, trimmed of all fat. Then butterfly by slicing the eye down the center lengthwise, without cutting all the way through the meat. Lay the slices of prosciutto in the center of the meat; then add thin strips of cheese. Close the lamb around the prosciutto and cheese and tie securely with string, overlapping the meat slightly so that the cheese does not melt out. Season stuffed meat with salt and pepper. In a skillet, melt just enough butter to cover the pan and cook the lamb over low fire, turning constantly, for about 15 minutes until brown and desired degree of rareness. Remove lamb from pan to a hot platter. Add marsala to skillet and simmer until reduced to one-third over medium heat. Add consomme and simmer until sauce is thick. Add brandy and serve sauce over the lamb.

ZUPPA INGLESSE

Serves Six to Eight
4 egg yolks
1 teaspoon flour
2 cups half-and-half
4 tablespoons granulated sugar
4 squares sweetened chocolate
2 dozen ladyfingers
mixed Italian liqueurs

In the top of a double boiler, but not over heat, beat eggs, add sugar and flour and continue beating until thick and creamy. In another pan, bring half-and-half to the boiling point. Place egg mixture over hot water and slowly add the hot half-and-half, beating constantly, until thick and creamy. Place half of the cream mixture in a pan of cold water and allow to cool. To the other half of the cream mixture add melted chocolate, mix well and allow to cool. Line the bottom of a deep, flat-bottomed serving dish with ladyfingers. (A pyrex 5 x 8 loaf dish works nicely.) Sprinkle the ladyfingers generously with assorted liqueurs until saturated. For this you may use a mixture of triple sec and cognac, pre-mixed Italian liqueurs, or any others you wish. Spread one layer of the natural cream mixture over these; top with another layer of the chocolate cream; then add another layer of ladyfingers; soak with liqueurs; add another layer of ice cream, etc. until all the ingredients are used. Chill for at least 12 hours before serving.

SCAMPI

Serves Four
12 Danish baby lobster tails
1 garlic clove, minced
clarified butter
2 ounces white wine
1 ounce lemon juice
parsley, chopped
dash of worcestershire sauce
dash of tabasco sauce
2 tablespoons whole butter

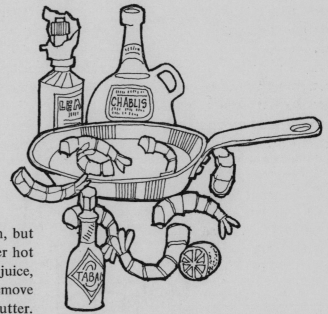

Remove the shells from the lobster and devein, but leave on the tails. Sauté in clarified butter over hot flame. Add minced garlic, white wine, lemon juice, parsley, worcestershire and tabasco sauce. Remove from fire and mix with two tablespoons whole butter.

VEAL PICCATA

Serves Four
12 very thin slices veal
    tenderloin
flour
clarified butter
2 jiggers dry white wine
1 jigger lemon juice
capers to taste
2 tablespoons whole butter

Pound veal very thin and dust with flour. In heavy skillet sauté veal briskly and fast in clarified butter. Add white wine, lemon juice, and capers. Let wine reduce. Add several tablespoons whole butter to finish.

STRAWBERRIES RUGGERO

Per serving
fresh strawberries
juice of ½ orange
1/2 jigger kirsch
1 jigger grand marnier
1 tablespoon sugar

Wash strawberries, remove stems and chill. Mix other ingredients together; add to strawberries and toss gently but well.

FETTUCCINE ALLA ROMANA

Serves Four
1/4 pound butter, softened
1/4 cup heavy cream
1/2 cup freshly grated parmesan cheese
1 tablespoon salt
yolk of one egg
1 pound fresh fettuccine
salt and pepper

Homemade Fettuccine Pasta
1 pound all-purpose flour, sifted
3 eggs
1 teaspoon salt
water

The secret of a good fettuccine is homemade fresh noodles which in most large cities can be obtained at Italian delicatessans or pasta factories. Dried fettuccine is not recommended. To prepare beat the butter until creamy and fluffy. Slowly add the egg yolk and cream, beating constantly; then beat in the grated cheese, a few tablespoons at a time. In a large pan, bring 8 quarts of water to a boil; add salt; and very gently drop in the fettuccine. Stir with a wooden fork for a few moments to separate the noodles and cook for about 7 minutes or until tender. The pasta should be "al dente;" not too cooked. Drain the fettuccine into a colander; and place in a large heated serving bowl. Add the creamed butter and cheese to the fettucine; toss very gently; season generously.

Pour the flour onto a pastry board, making a well in the center. Place eggs and salt in the well and mix quickly with your fingers until you have a rough ball. Add a little water until you have a firm ball. Knead with your fingers for ten to fifteen minutes, adding extra flour if the dough seems sticky. The dough should be smooth and elastic. Cover the dough with a bowl and let it rest about 20 minutes. Divide the dough into three or four pieces and roll out as thinly as possible on a lightly floured board. Sprinkle the rolled-out dough lightly with flour and cut into strips about one-half inch wide. Spread on a cloth and let dry for about an hour before cooking.

ZABAIONE

Per Serving
2 egg yolks
3 teaspoons sugar
2 ounces dry marsala wine

In the top of a double boiler, beat eggs and sugar with a wire whisk until thick. Beat in the wine. Then place over boiling water and beat vigorously until hot, very thick and foamy. Serve immediately.

LAZYMAN'S CIOPPINO

Serves Four
1½ pounds crab meat, cooked
4 large oysters
8 scallops
8 prawns, shelled and deveined
tomato sauce, below
french bread

This is an easy version of the classic fisherman's stew of San Francisco, introduced by the Italians. Simply cook all the fish in the sauce for about five minutes and serve in bowls with plenty of french bread. The sauce, of course, may be made ahead of time and keeps well.

Tomato Sauce for Four
1/2 medium onion, chopped
1 small garlic clove, chopped
1 pinch oregano
1 bay leaf
1 pinch sage
2 No. 2½ cans solid pack tomatoes
1 tablespoon tomato paste
1/4 cup water
salt and pepper to taste

Sauté onion and garlic in olive oil until soft. Add spices and cook awhile longer. Add tomatoes, tomato paste, water, salt and pepper and simmer for one hour. Strain before using.

CRAB LEGS SAUTÉ

Serves Four
2 pounds fresh crab legs
4 tablespoons chopped onion
2 garlic cloves, minced
1 tablespoon butter
1 tablespoon olive oil
4 mushrooms, sliced
dash MSG
1/4 cup white wine
chopped parsley
lemon wedges

Remove shells from crab legs. Sauté onion and garlic in mixture of the butter and oil until tender. Add mushrooms. When mushrooms are soft, add crab legs, MSG and wine. Simmer a few minutes and serve sprinkled with chopped parsley and garnished with a lemon wedge. It is important to use fresh crab legs advises Scoma's chef, Salvador Patané.

BRODETTO

Serves Six
2 pounds white fish, boned and fileted
3 pounds finely chopped onions
flour
2 jiggers white wine, *very* dry
3/4 cup tomato sauce
olive oil

In heavy skillet, sauté onions in olive oil over medium heat until tender and yellow. Dredge fish in flour and simmer in onion mixture for four minutes on one side and three minutes on the other side. Add wine and simmer another two minutes. Add tomato sauce and simmer, covered, for four to five minutes longer. This is the creation of Tana's chef Alfonso.

CHICKEN FLORENTINE

Serves Four
4 whole chicken breasts
2 beaten eggs
flour and salt
vegetable oil
1½ pounds fresh spinach
butter
4 ounces mozarella cheese
grated parmesan cheese
3 jiggers dry white wine
juice of ½ lemon
4 jiggers chicken broth

Remove bones and skin from chicken; dredge in salted flour; dip in beaten eggs and sauté in vegetable oil over low flame for ten minutes on each side. (Use a pan which can be later placed in the oven.) Meanwhile cook the fresh spinach; drain; chop and add butter. Top the sautéed chicken with spinach, sprinkle liberally with parmesan cheese and place sliced mozarella over this. Bake for 10 to 12 minutes in preheated 350° oven. Remove chicken to heated platter in warming oven. In pan in which chicken was cooked, add wine and lemon juice and simmer until wine is reduced to half. Add chicken broth and simmer another two minutes. Pour sauce on chicken.

SPAGHETTI ALLA CARBONARA

Serves Four

6 ounces Italian bacon (pancetta,
   unsmoked) diced
4 green onions, chopped
1 tablespoon olive oil
6 tablespoons white wine
3 large eggs
3 ounces grated parmesan cheese
2 tablespoons chopped parsley
1/2 teaspoon black pepper
1 pound spaghetti

Saute bacon in olive oil in heavy aluminum pan for
two minutes over low fire. (If you cannot buy the
Italian bacon, Canadian bacon may be substituted.)
Add onions and sauté for three more minutes. Add
wine and cook until evaporated. In a large bowl mix
eggs, cheese, parsley and pepper and beat a few
seconds. Cook spaghetti in one gallon boiling, salted
water until tender. Drain spaghetti and pour into
bowl with egg mixture. Add the hot pancetta sauce,
mix well and serve at once. Chef Giovanni Leoni, who
brought this recipe from Rome, stresses the impor-
tance of timing the spaghetti so that it and the sauce
are ready at the same time.

VEAL CUTLET MODENESE

Serves Four
4 5-ounce slices veal
2 whole eggs
1/4 cup grated parmesan cheese
1 tablespoon chopped parsley
1 cup breadcrumbs
salt, pepper
olive oil
4 ½-ounce slices prosciutto ham
4 1-ounce slices monterey jack cheese
3/4 cup bechamel sauce (see index)

Have your butcher slice and pound the veal. Combine eggs, a small pinch of salt and pepper, cheese and parsley. Mix well. Soak veal in egg mixture, then dip in breadcrumbs until completely covered. Press cutlets between your hands or with a wide knife blade and deep-fry over hot flame in oil until golden. Remove cutlets from oil and drain on absorbent paper. Place half of the bechamel sauce in a baking dish and place cutlets in dish. Pour remaining sauce over cutlets and place one slice of prosciutto and one slice of cheese on each cutlet with the cheese on top. Bake at 375° for ten minutes. Veal Princessa, a variation of this dish, may be made by substituting cooked asparagus and parmesan cheese for the prosciutto and monterey jack.

JOE VANESSI'S SPECIAL

Serves Four
1 bunch fresh spinach
2 ounces olive oil
4 tablespoons butter
6 green onions
1½ pounds ground beef
8 eggs
1/2 cup grated parmesan cheese
salt and pepper

Wash spinach very well and cook in as little water as possible for 8 minutes. Drain and chop very fine. In a skillet, sauté the well chopped onions until they begin to color in the butter and oil. Add meat and mix with fork to break up chunks of meat; cook until the meat juices in the bottom of the pan are dry. Add spinach and mix well. Add eggs, cheese, salt and pepper and mix with a spatula, being careful not to let the eggs stick to the bottom of the pan. Cook for about four minutes, mixing constantly.

CHICKEN SAUTÉ ALLA VANESSI

Serves Four
4—5 pounds chicken serving pieces
1/4 cup olive oil
2 medium onions, quartered
2 green peppers, sliced
2 cloves, garlic, chopped
5 sage leaves
1 sprig rosemary
1/4 cup white wine
salt and pepper

Sauté chicken in a heavy bottom pan in the oil until golden. Add garlic, onions, pepper, sage and rosemary and sauté slowly until the vegetables start to cook. Add salt, pepper and wine and cook slowly for 25 minutes. If wine and vegetable juices evaporate during cooking, add a few ounces of chicken broth.

The Gold Rush also lured many adventurers from the Central European countries, but there was no great second wave of immigration to California in the 19th century as there was from Italy. Thus the Germanic and the Austro-Hungarian culinary traditions have been minor in California, and there are few good German or Hungarian restaurants.

A notable exception is Schroeder's, which has served consistently fine and authentic German food since the 1890's, and whose recipes are included in the following pages. In the 1950's and 1960's, a number of expertly trained German and Swiss chefs have come to California, but ironically, most of them are to be found in restaurants specializing in a wide range of continental food, such as Rolf's whose recipes are also included in this section. One of the finest examples of the Austro-Hungarian cuisine is to be found at Manka's Czech Restuarant in Inverness. There are other German recipes included in the international section of this book.

PIROSHKI

Makes One Dozen
1 pound ground beef
1 large onion, chopped
1 small garlic clove, minced
1 tablespoon cooking oil
1/3 cup parsley chopped
1½ cups sweet and sour cabbage
bread dough for one standard
   size loaf (white)
egg white

Use your favorite bread dough recipe or substitute frozen bread dough or hot roll mix. Prepare dough and allow to rise once. To make the filling sauté onion and garlic in oil until limp. Add ground beef and brown lightly, stirring to break up any lumps. Remove from fire and pour off excess oil. Add parsley, cabbage, salt and pepper to taste. Break off a piece of the risen dough about the size of a walnut and roll out into a thin circle. Place a heaping tablespoon of the filling on the circle; fold in half and pinch edges together well to seal in filling. Piroshki should have plump centers with tapering ends. Place seam side down on a lightly greased baking sheet and let rise in a warm place for about an hour. Brush with egg white and bake at 350° for 15 minutes until browned.

ROAST DUCK POLONAISE

Serves Six
2 4-pound ducklings, cleaned
salt and pepper
thyme
4 ounces golden raisins
4 ounces pitted prunes
6 ounces dried apricots
2½ tablespoons granulated sugar
2½ tablespoons vinegar
1 quart chicken stock
1 ounce Madeira wine

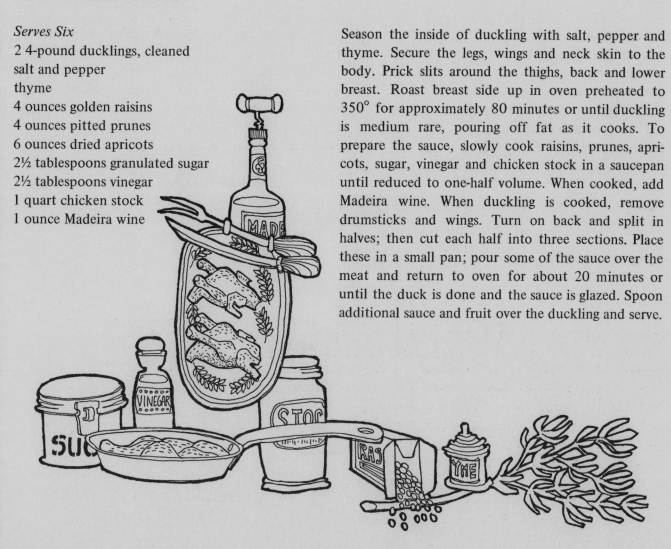

Season the inside of duckling with salt, pepper and thyme. Secure the legs, wings and neck skin to the body. Prick slits around the thighs, back and lower breast. Roast breast side up in oven preheated to 350° for approximately 80 minutes or until duckling is medium rare, pouring off fat as it cooks. To prepare the sauce, slowly cook raisins, prunes, apricots, sugar, vinegar and chicken stock in a saucepan until reduced to one-half volume. When cooked, add Madeira wine. When duckling is cooked, remove drumsticks and wings. Turn on back and split in halves; then cut each half into three sections. Place these in a small pan; pour some of the sauce over the meat and return to oven for about 20 minutes or until the duck is done and the sauce is glazed. Spoon additional sauce and fruit over the duckling and serve.

CASSATA

Twelve Servings
1 small package almonds
4 tablespoons butter
3/4 cup raisins, chopped
1 quart high quality vanilla ice cream
1 pint chocolate ice cream
151 proof rum (or rum extract)
maraschino cherries

Sauté almonds in butter until nicely toasted. Soften vanilla ice cream (but do not melt) and add raisins, almonds and rum to taste, mixing well but very quickly. Fill loaf pan three-quarters full and freeze until firm. When ice cream is hard, soften chocolate ice cream and fill the loaf pan over the frozen vanilla mixture. Freeze until hard. To serve, unmold cassata on small cutting board and decorate the top with a center row of halved maraschino cherries. Slice into pieces 3/4 inch thick. Leftover cassata may be kept very well in freezer.

CARAWAY SEED SOUP

Makes Four Cups
4 cups veal and/or chicken stock
6 tablespoons butter
1/4 cup diced vegetables (onion,
    carrot, celery)
1/2 teaspoon caraway seeds
chopped parsley
salt and pepper
3 tablespoons flour
1/4 cup table cream

Dice the vegetables into small pieces and brown in 4 tablespoons butter. Add the caraway seeds and stock and bring to a gentle boil. Meanwhile blend 3 tablespoons flour into 2 tablespoons melted butter and cook over low heat, stirring constantly until lightly browned and thick. Press the flour and butter roux through a fine strainer; blend in the cream; stir until thick; add to soup and bring to a second boil. Adjust heat so that a slow simmer is maintained and cook for approximately 30 minutes more. Add salt, pepper and chopped parsley to taste, and serve.

VEAL PAPRIKASH

Serves Four
1½ pounds veal shoulder or leg (boned)
salt
1 teaspoon paprika
4 tablespoons butter
4 tablespoons chopped onions
2 tablespoons flour
2 medium tomatoes, pulverized
1/2 cup sour cream (or heavy cream)
chicken stock

Cut veal into bite-size cubes. Next brown the onions in the butter. Add paprika and cook for one minute. Add veal cubes; sprinkle with salt; and stir until coated with onion and paprika mixture. Cover pan and stew slowly for 30 to 45 minutes. When stewed, sprinkle the veal with flour; raise heat; and stir until slightly browned. Add enough chicken stock to make a sauce. Add tomatoes, which have been run through a sieve or blender, and simmer until the veal is tender. Before serving add cream, salt to taste and heat until nearly boiling. Serve with rice or over noodles.

LEMON TORT

Meringue Base
5 egg whites
1½ cups granulated sugar
butter

Beat the egg whites, slowly adding half of the sugar, until stiff. Then gently fold in the remaining sugar. Spread into two ten-inch cake pans, which have been generously buttered. (Or, using a pastry bag, you may pipe the meringue into two torts, ten-inches in diameter, on a well buttered cookie sheet.) Bake in a slow oven (250°) for one hour. Allow to cool.

Lemon Creme
8 egg yolks
1/2 cup lemon juice
4 teaspoons lemon rind
1½ cups granulated sugar
2 teaspoons vanilla extract
whipping cream
semi-sweet dark chocolate

Combine egg yolks, lemon juice, sugar and lemon rind in the top of a double boiler. Cook slowly, stirring frequently until thick. Remove from heat and cool slightly; then add vanilla. When the creme is completely cooled, spread it on both layers of meringue. Place one layer on top of the other and decorate the top layer with sweetened whipped cream and slivers of chocolate.

CHEF HEINZ' LENTIL SOUP

Serves Four to Five
1 quart ham stock (see below)
1 medium ham hock
1 cup lentils
1 bay leaf
1 teaspoon chopped parsley
1 teaspoon chopped celery leaves
1/2 teaspoon thyme
3 bacon strips, cut fine
flour
2 skinless frankfurters, diced
1/2 cup sour cream
1 teaspoon red wine vinegar
salt, white pepper and nutmeg

Ham Stock

2 pounds ham bone and fat
10 bay leaves
2 carrots, sliced
2 branches celery, chopped
2 leeks, chopped
1 medium onion, chopped
5 whole cloves
1 tablespoon beef extract
2 quarts water
Simmer ingredients for two to three hours. Skim of fat and strain.

Make a bouquet garni of the bay leaf, parsley, celery and thyme (tie in a cheesecloth bag). Wash lentils well and soak overnight in ham stock (beef stock may be substituted, but ham stock is preferable). Cook the bacon and onions until slightly browned. Add enough flour to the bacon fat to make a smooth paste. Add lentils and stock to paste, slowly on medium fire, stirring constantly to insure a smooth consistency. Add pieces of ham from the ham hock, frankfurters, ham bone and bouquet garni and simmer until lentils are tender. When ready to serve, remove ham bone and bouquet garni. Then take a ladle of soup from the pot and mix with the sour cream with a whisk until smooth. Then slowly add the sour cream to the soup pot, stirring constantly. Add vinegar and season to taste. As the ham stock tends to be salty, no additional salt may be needed.

CHEF HEINZ' ROQUEFORT DRESSING

Makes 4½ cups
6 ounces Roquefort cheese, finely crumbled
3 tablespoons white vinegar
1 cup olive oil
1 tablespoon prepared mustard
1/4 teaspoon garlic salt
1/4 teaspoon onion salt
1/4 teaspoon cayenne
1/4 teaspoon paprika
1/2 teaspoon worcestershire sauce
1 teaspoon lemon juice
1 teaspoon ground oregano
2 cups mayonnaise

Put vinegar in bowl and slowly add olive oil while beating with a whisk or electric mixer. Add mustard, seasoning and spices and continue beating. Add cheese and continue beating. Add mayonnaise and beat until smooth and thick. Add salt and pepper to taste.

EPINARDS A LA CHEF HEINZ

Serves Eight
3 pounds fresh spinach
2 tablespoons melted butter
2 hardboiled eggs, chopped
1 teaspoon MSG

Wash spinach leaves and parboil in salted, boiling water for two to five minutes. Cool under running water and squeeze dry to extract all moisture. Chop fine and sauté quickly in melted butter. Combine with sauce, add MSG, correct seasoning and simmer three to five minutes. Serve in casserole with chopped egg sprinkled on top.

Sauce for Epinards
1/4 pound butter
1/2 cup flour
1 cup half-and-half
1/2 teaspoon allspice
1/4 teaspoon ground nutmeg
1/4 teaspoon ground cloves
1/4 teaspoon cinnamon
1/4 teaspoon white pepper
1 teaspoon brown sugar
salt to taste

Let butter soften and knead with sifted flour into a smooth paste. Bring half-and-half to the boiling point and add all other ingredients except the flour and butter. Simmer for three minutes. Slowly stir flour and butter paste into the milk until smooth. If sauce is too thick, add a little hot milk.

RED CABBAGE GERMAN STYLE

Serves Eight
4 pounds red cabbage
2 cups boiling chicken or beef broth
4 tablespoons butter
2 tablespoons vinegar
2 apples, peeled and chopped
2 whole cloves
3 ounces red wine
1 tablespoon sugar
salt and pepper to taste
1/2 stick cinnamon

Remove wilted leaves from cabbage. Cut head in half and remove center. Shred cabbage very fine; pour boiling broth over it; add butter and simmer for 1 hour. Then add remaining ingredients except wine and continue cooking for 1/2 hour, turning frequently. Add wine and cook another ten minutes. The cooked cabbage should be neither too sour nor too sweet.

SCHROEDER'S SAUERBRATEN

Serves Eight
5 pound top round roast of beef
2 cups vinegar
4 cups water
whole mixed spices (4 bay leaves, 3 cloves,
    12 peppercorns, 1/2 teaspoon thyme,
    pinch mustard seed)
1 large onion, sliced
salt to taste
2 tablespoons sugar
1/4 cup chopped celery and carrots (optional)
3 tablespoons flour
2 tablespoons shortening
3 ounces red wine
dash nutmeg (optional)
dash paprika (optional)

Tie up the mixed spices in a cheesecloth bag. Then heat, but do not boil, the vinegar, water, spices, onion and a little salt. Place the roast in a crock (not metal); pour the vinegar solution over it, adding water if meat is not completely covered; place the spice bag in the crock; and marinate the meat for two to three days in the refrigerator, turning frequently. When ready to cook, remove the meat from the pickling solution and sear it on all sides in hot shortening. Remove the meat to a roasting pan; sauté the celery and carrots in the fat; brown 3 tablespoons of flour in the fat; add spices from the pickling solution and several cups of the pickling solution and the sugar and simmer a few minutes. Pour the sauce over the roast; cover pan; and bake from 2½ to 3 hours in a moderate oven (350°). Turn and baste frequently. One-half hour before the meat is done, add the wine. When cooked, remove meat to a hot platter and strain the sauce into a saucepan, and thicken with flour and water paste to make a gravy. Correct seasoning with nutmeg, paprika, and salt. If sauce is not sour enough add vinegar.

POTATO PANCAKES

Serves Eight
3 pounds potatoes
4 eggs
1¼ cups flour
1/2 tablespoon salt
pepper to taste
1/2 teaspoon grated onion
1 large sour apple, peeled and grated
shortening

Peel potatoes, wash and let stand in water. Remove from water and grate quickly; drain well; then mix in eggs, flour, pepper, salt, grated apple, and onion. In very hot shortening, cook 3 or 4 *thin* pancakes at a time until brown and crisp. Do not cover them before serving.

We have grouped the following Armenian, Yugoslavian and Greek recipes together, because of the inter-relationship of many Eastern Mediterranean foods. Other Greek and Armenian dishes complement any of these recipes nicely.

The immigration from the Eastern European countries to California during the 19th century was small, compared with the numbers who came from Western Europe, and thus the influence on the California cuisine was relatively minor.

Many of the Greeks who did immigrate in the 1800's joined the Italians in the fishing industry and others did open restaurants, but the menus were quite limited. In this century, the famed Omar Khayam's in San Francisco helped to popularize Armenian food.

The three restaurants whose recipes we have included here are doing an extraordinary job today of introducing a broad spectrum of sophisticated dishes from the Eastern Mediterranean to Californians. Peter Zane's L'Odeon, which opened in the late 1960's, brings Greek *haute cuisine* to Caliornia for the first time; Harry Akulian's Haji Baba gives the highest standards of quality and service to Armenian fare; and Bob Sipovak's Adriatic offers a wide range of dishes from all parts of Yugoslavia.

CHEE KUFTA (LAMB TARTARE)

Serves Four as Appetizer
1 cup ground lamb (see below)
1 cup fine bulghour (see below)
1 small onion, chopped fine
1/3 cup bell pepper, chopped fine
1/3 cup fresh parsley, chopped fine
1/3 cup green onion, chopped fine
1 cup cold water
salt and pepper to taste
pinch cayenne
pinch cumin

As this dish is served uncooked, it is very important that top quality lamb be used (Haji Baba uses only prime). Have your butcher completely defat meat from the round of the leg. It is preferable to grind it yourself, three times, *just before serving*, to savor the true flavor of Chee Kufta. Bulghour is a cracked wheat, available at most health food stores and Armenian markets. To prepare the dish, grind the lamb and mix with salt, pepper, cayenne and cumin. Add the bulghour, all of the chopped onion and only 1 tablespoon each of the green pepper, parsley and green onion. Knead by grasping a handful of the mixture and squeezing it. As it is forced out of your hand, knead it with the palm of your other hand. While kneading, sprinkle a little cold water on the mixture every minute for about 10 minutes, until the mixture becomes homogenized and moist. Then grasp one-ounce portions (two tablespoons) of the mixture in your fist to form small cylinder-shaped pieces on which the impression of your fingers is very prominent. Continue this until all the mixture is used and place the meat cylinders around the edge of a serving dish. Place the remaining portion of the chopped vegetables in the center of the dish and serve immediately. (The freshness is the secret of Chee Kufta.) Dip meat into chopped vegetables and dine.

KOUZOUT-KZARTMA (LAMB SHANKS)

Serves Four
4 lamb shanks cut in half
1 small can tomato paste
2 fresh tomatoes, diced
2 stalks celery, chopped
1/2 bell pepper, chopped
1 onion, chopped
3 bay leaves
1 teaspoon salt
1 teaspoon white pepper
1 teaspoon paprika
1 teaspoon savory salt

Rinse lamb shanks, cutting off achilles tendon. Place in baking pan large enough so that all shanks lay flat on the bottom. Fill pan with enough cold water to cover tops of lamb shanks. Sprinkle all remaining ingredients into the water. Bake for 2½ to 3 hours in a 350° oven.

CHEESE BUREK

Serves Eight to Ten
1 pound hoop cheese
1/2 pound feta cheese
1 pint cottage cheese
1 cup butter, melted
4 whole eggs
1 teaspoon sugar
1 pound dough leaves

The paper thin dough leaves (same as used for strudel or baklava) may be purchased at Greek or Armenian bakeries or import shops. Ricotta cheese may be substituted for hoop cheese, but use only half as much. To make the stuffing, mix all the cheese together. In another bowl, beat the eggs with the sugar and fold them into the cheese mixture. Stir well until creamy. Take one dough sheet (about 8 x 10 inches) and sprinkle melted butter on it. Then sprinkle about two tablespoons of the cheese mixture evenly over the dough. Roll the dough lengthwise into a long, narrow tube. Roll the tube into a snail-shaped coil, so that you have a circular roll about 3 to 4 inches in diameter. Repeat process until you have used the filling. Place the bureks in a greased baking pan and bake for 15 minutes at 350°.

MEAT BUREK

Serves Eight to Ten
1½ pounds beef and veal, minced
3 onions, chopped
1/2 cup melted beef fat
salt and pepper
2 eggs
1 tablespoons olive or vegetable oil
1 pound dough leaves

Sauté onions in oil until tender; then add the meat and fry it with the onions until all the liquid has been absorbed. Remove from fire; season with salt and pepper; add the eggs and mix well. To make the bureks, follow the same process as cheese bureks, using melted fat instead of butter. Place in greased pan and bake for 25 minutes at 400°.

MUSAKA

Serves Six
2 large eggplants
salt
3/4 cup vegetable and olive oil mixed
1/2 onion, chopped
1½ tomatoes, diced
1/2 green pepper, chopped
1 tablespoon parsley, chopped fine
pepper
6 eggs
1/4 pound pork or veal, minced
1/4 pound beef, minced
1¼ cups milk
flour

Peel the eggplant and cut into thin slices. Salt and let stand. Sauté onions and tomatoes in two tablespoons oil. Add minced meat and sauté. Add green pepper and parsley. Press each slice of eggplant between the palms of your hands and wipe it dry. Dust each slice of eggplant with flour, dip into three lightly beaten eggs and fry in remaining oil. Oil an ovenproof dish; approximately 9x13, and arrange the eggplant and minced meat in layers, beginning and ending with the eggplant. Beat three eggs, add milk, and pour over the Musaka. Bake in a moderate oven (350°) for approximately 1 hour until a nice crust forms on the top.

XERXIS (CUCUMBER AND YOGURT SOUP)

Makes Six cups
3 cucumbers, peeled and seeded
1 onion
1 garlic clove
2 pints yogurt
1 cup sour cream
4 teaspoons fresh dill weed
pinch salt and pepper

Grate onion and cucumber (or run through blender).
Add crushed garlic and other ingredients and mix
well. Chill before serving.

LAMB STEW PILAF

Serves Four
1½ pounds lean lamb, cut in small pieces
1/2 cup butter or oil
1/2 pound onions, chopped
1/2 cup tomato paste
1/8 teaspoon cinnamon
salt and pepper to taste
2 cups water

Sauté half of the onions in butter until golden brown. Add the meat and cook for ten minutes, stirring constantly. Add the rest of the onions and tomato paste diluted with the water. Bring to boil; reduce heat; season with salt, pepper and cinnamon; and simmer uncovered until the meat is cooked and the sauce is reduced. Serve meat and sauce over rice pilaf, below.

Rice Pilaf
1 cup rice
2 cups water or chicken stock
1/3 cup butter
salt and pepper to taste

Rinse and drain the rice. Bring stock (or water) and butter to boil; add salt and pepper. When liquid is simmering add rice; stir well with wooden spoon; reduce heat to very low; cover and cook for about half an hour. When cooked, add more butter; stir lightly; and separate rice grains with a fork.

San Francisco

CRÊPES AEGEAN

Serves Four
5 ounces crushed pistachio nuts
1/2 pint whipping cream
1 teaspoon sugar
2 jiggers Metaxa cognac
1 jigger ouzo liqueur
8 crêpes (see index for recipe)
2 tablespoons butter
1 tablespoon honey

Beat whipping cream until *very* stiff with 1/2 jigger cognac and 1/2 jigger ouzo and sugar. Place a heaping tablespoon of whipped cream mixture in center of each crêpe. Fold one side of crêpe over cream; then fold each adjoining side; finally roll crêpe so that the final roll is sealed on three sides. (Fold loosely and lightly so that cream does not flow out of folded crêpe.) In a chafing dish, melt butter and add honey. Cook until blended and honey is melted. Add 1½ jiggers cognac and 1/2 jigger ouzo and flame. When fire dies, place stuffed crêpes in pan and bathe in the sauce. Serve crêpes and spoon sauce over them.

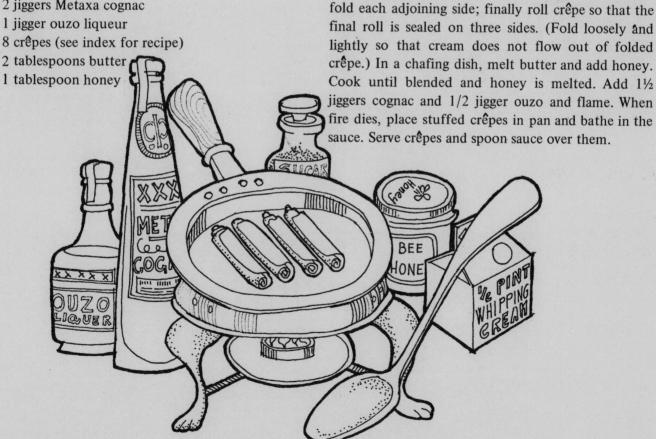

Frenchmen came to California before the Gold Rush and started orchards and wineries, and gold fever attracted more. As fortunes were amassed in California, French food became a status symbol and some of the most sophisticated *haute cuisine* outside of Paris was found in San Francisco. At a now legendary banquet for Senator William Sharon in 1876 at the Palace Hotel, eleven intricate Gallic dishes were served with nine French wines! Although some of the oldest restaurants in California are French, the French influence on the California cuisine waned in the early 1900's. In the last decade, however, the appreciation of Gallic food and the number of fine French restaurants has increased tremendously.

Rules of French cooking could fill an encyclopaedia, but we hope the following tips will be of some help. As the sauce is all-important in French food, a small investment in a French whisk will pay great dividends in results and ease in making your sauces. Also select the size of your cooking pan with care to match your proportions, as the sauce will cook away in an oversize skillet. The French cook with sweet butter almost exclusively. Burned butter will ruin the flavor. It is the fat that burns, so clarify your butter before you saute and never put butter in a hot pan; heat the pan and butter together.

Please do forget the old addage about "cooking wines," and use good wines. Wine and brandy are used for flavor, not for the alcoholic content which evaporates anyway; and the better the wine, the better the flavor. Select your table wines with care to complement each dish; the type of wine used to prepare the dish is usually a good choice.

TOMATOES AND MUSHROOMS SALAD

Serves Four
4 ripe tomatoes
8 large fresh white mushrooms
8 "chapons" (small breadcrusts
   rubbed with garlic)
1 squeeze of lemon juice
salt
basic salad dressing (see below)

Peel tomatoes, remove seeds, and cut in quartered sections. Cut mushrooms in fine slices and season with salt and lemon juice. Mix in bowl with dressing and herbs. Serve on cold plates.

Basic Salad Dressing
2/3 cup imported olive oil
1/3 cup red wine vinegar
1 teaspoon imported white wine mustard
salt
white pepper
fresh ground black pepper
green onions, chopped fine
parsley, chopped fine
fresh basil

This is the basic dressing for all salads served at Charles' Restaurant. In your salad bowl, mix salt, white pepper, and mustard. Add oil first (important) and mix. Add vinegar and blend to a smooth mixture. Add the ingredients of the salad. Add black pepper and mix again. Add herbs, mix again, and serve. The secret of this recipe is that it must be fresh, prepared no more than ten minutes before you intend to serve it, and mixed very thoroughly.

BROILED RACK OF LAMB BÉARNAISE

Per serving
1 rack of lamb
salt
black pepper
ground thyme
sage
butter

The racks should be chosen from a tender, aged loin. Each individual serving should include from 4 to 5 chops. All fat and nerves must be removed as the racks have to be lean. Season with salt, black pepper, ground thyme, and sage. Brush with butter and broil on both sides on the grill until medium-rare. Overcooked lamb will loose its juice and tenderness. Each rack of lamb is served covered with Béarnaise Sauce.

Béarnaise Sauce
Makes one cup
1 teaspoon fresh shallots, chopped fine
2 teaspoons fresh tarragon leaves,
    chopped fine
salt
dash of thyme
1/2 teaspoon ground coarse black pepper
4 raw egg yolks
1 teaspoon cold water
1/2 pound butter
1/2 lemon
1/2 glass red wine vinegar
1/2 glass dry white wine
dash of cayenne pepper

In a pan mix shallots, tarragon, and spices. Add vinegar and wine; simmer and reduce to one third of quantity. Cool. Add the egg yolks and cold water, and over steam slowly beat the mixture. While beating slowly add the melted butter and keep beating until the consistency of smooth cream. Correct seasoning and add dash of cayenne pepper and lemon juice. Keep lukewarm.

SURPRISE LAMB CHOPS

Serves Four
12 lean lamb chops, trimmed
2 slices ham, diced fine
1 small chicken breast, diced fine
2 large mushrooms, chopped fine
2 cloves shallots, chopped fine
pinch thyme
salt and pepper
2 leaves fresh tarragon, chopped
1 cup dry white wine
4 ounces puff pastry dough
butter

(Note: you may buy the puff pastry or strudell dough at fine bakeries or gourmet specialty shops; this is recommended unless you are very adept at making your own.) Sauté the ham, chicken, mushroom and shallots in butter; season with salt, pepper and thyme; and remove from fire when half cooked. Simmer tarragon leaves and freshly ground black pepper in 1/2 cup of the wine until the wine is reduced. Mix the cooked tarragon and wine into the meat mixture; add another 1/2 cup wine and finish cooking the chopped meat. Roll out the dough until paper thin and cut into pieces approximately 4 inches square (three per lamb chop if you use strudell dough leaves). Season lamb chops on both sides and grill to rare only. Let chops cool slightly; then cover each chop on one side with the sauteed meat mixture and wrap with a square of dough. Brush with butter and cook in medium oven for ten minutes, until dough is cooked to a golden color.

SPINACH SALAD FLAMBÉ

Serves Six
2 bunches fresh tender spinach
white vinegar
8 strips bacon
4 tablespoons sugar
4 tablespoons wine vinegar
1 tablespoon worcestershire sauce
1 lemon
1 jigger cognac
watercress

Remove stems from spinach leaves; wash in cold water to which a little vinegar has been added; and dry well. Place leaves in salad bowl with some watercress. Cut bacon into 1/2 inch squares and sauté in a chafing dish until cooked. Add sugar, wine vinegar and worcestershire sauce. Heat to a boil and strain sauce over spinach leaves, leaving bacon in chafing dish. Squeeze lemon over leaves and toss until wilted. Drain dressing off the salad and place the spinach leaves on plates. Add cognac to the bacon, ignite and spoon over the spinach. Serve at once.

BREAST OF CHICKEN IN CURRY

Serves Six
6 large chicken breasts
1 cup chopped onions
1 cup chopped celery
1/2 cup chopped apple
2 bananas
shredded coconut
3 pineapple slices
pineapple juice
curry powder
salt and pepper
2 cups chicken stock
1/2 cup dry white wine
sweet butter
flour
1/2 pint whipping cream

Curry Sauce
Sauté onions, celery, apples and one sliced banana in sweet butter. Add curry powder to taste and chicken stock and bring to a boil. In another pan blend three tablespoons flour with three tablespoons melted butter and stir into sauce. Add salt and pepper and correct curry seasoning. Simmer for two hours and strain.

Preparation of Chicken
Bone and skin chicken breasts and dust with flour. Sprinkle to taste with salt, pepper and curry powder. Sauté the breasts in butter until golden, not brown. Add wine, about 1/3 of the curry sauce, pineapple slices and sliced banana and simmer for 15 minutes. Place chicken breasts in a deep platter and garnish with the pineapple and bananas. Whip cream; blend gently into remaining curry sauce and pour over the chicken. Glaze quickly under broiler. Sprinkle with browned shredded coconut. Serve with rice pilaf and chutney.

BANANA VIRGINIA

Serves Four
4 bananas, peeled
2 lemons
1/2 cup brown sugar
dash granulated sugar
juice of two oranges
nutmeg
cinnamon
sweet butter
1 jigger banana liqueur
1 jigger rum
vanilla ice cream

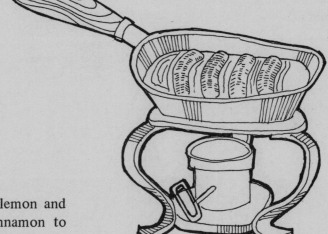

Preparation of Syrup
Combine orange juice with juice of one lemon and brown sugar. Heat, add nutmeg and cinnamon to taste and set aside.

Preparation of Bananas
Melt just enough sweet butter to cover bottom of skillet or chafing dish. Sauté both sides of bananas over medium heat and sprinkle with sugar and a little lemon juice. Add syrup and simmer for one minute. Add banana liqueur and rum and ignite. Serve with ice cream.

SPINACH AND LEEK SOUP

Serves Six
1 cup minced onion
2½ cups diced potatoes
4 cups chicken or turkey broth
1 cup frozen peas (optional)
2 leeks
2 bunches of spinach
1 tablespoon butter
1/2 cup light cream
1/2 cup chopped parsley
1 pinch thyme
1 pinch ground sage
salt and pepper

Sauté onion, potatoes, peas, leeks, and spinach in butter for 20 to 25 minutes. Add broth, herbs, salt and pepper to taste, and simmer for another 30 minutes. Strain; add cream and reheat. Garnish with a little cooked, chopped spinach or chopped parsley. This amount fills six soup bowls or twelve boullion cups.

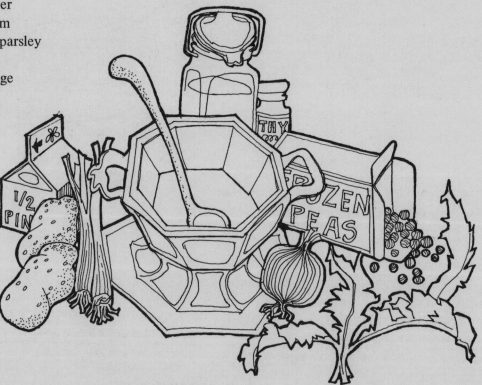

POULET DIPLOMAT

Serves Four
2½ to 3 pounds chicken
butter
3 shallots or 1/2 onion
1 leek, finely sliced
1 carrot, finely sliced
1 celery branch, finely sliced
1 garlic clove, minced
3 ounces dry sherry
1 cup sliced mushrooms
1/2 cup all-purpose cream
1 cup chicken broth
12 asparagus, cooked or canned
duchess potatoes or parboiled
  baby potatoes

Chez Gerard serves one-half chicken per person, cut into three serving pieces. We recommend that you buy precut pieces of breast and leg in sufficient quantity to serve four. Roll chicken in flour and pan fry it in butter until golden brown. Add sherry and ignite, shaking pan until the fire burns down. Add onions, celery, carrot, leek and garlic. Add broth, salt and pepper to taste, and cook slowly for 30 to 35 minutes. Remove chicken to a hot serving platter. Add cream to the sauce; stir quickly for a few minutes on a hot fire; then strain the sauce. Garnish the chicken with duchess potatoes or potato-balls, asparagus and mushrooms. Pour cream sauce over the dish and place under the broiler or in hot oven until golden brown. (Note: Duchess potatoes are made by combining two cups mashed potatoes with two egg yolks, butter and salt. Form into balls, brush with lightly beaten egg whites and brown in hot oven.)

CRÊPES TAJ MAHAL

Serves Six
12 French crêpes (see index)
curry shrimp filling (see below)
clam and wine sauce (see next page)
3 hard boiled eggs, quartered
12 mushroom caps
2 tablespoons slivered almonds
curry powder
1½ cups hollandaise sauce (see index)

Fill crêpes with curried shrimp mixture and roll evenly to keep in as much sauce as possible. Pour a layer of the clam and wine sauce into the bottom of a shallow baking dish; then place the crêpes in the pan. Garnish with eggs, mushroom caps and almonds; set aside. Blend hollandaise sauce into the remaining clam and wine sauce and ladle the combined sauces over the crêpes; sprinkle lightly with curry powder and bake uncovered in preheated oven at 350° for 30 to 35 minutes. This dish can be prepared in advance, even the preceeding day; refrigerated and baked when ready to serve.

Curry Shrimp Filling for 12 Crêpes

3 tablespoons finely chopped shallots
2 tablespoons cooking oil
1/3 cup dry white wine
1 tablespoon currant jelly
1/2 cup sliced fresh mushrooms
1/4 cup apple sauce
1 pound baby shrimp
1/2 cup cream or half-and-half
1/4 teaspoon salt
2–3 teaspoons curry powder
2 tablespoons slivered almonds
2 teaspoons cornstarch
1/4 cup water

Sauté shallots in oil; add wine and simmer several minutes. Add remaining ingredients except cornstarch and water, stirring constantly and simmer about five minutes. Dissolve cornstarch in water and stir into sauce. Stir over low heat until the sauce thickens.

Clam and Wine Sauce for Crêpes Taj Mahal

3 tablespoons melted butter
1/2 cup all-purpose flour
2 tablespoons shallots, finely chopped
2 tablespoons cooking oil
1½ cups dry white wine
1/2 teaspoon salt
1/4 teaspoon thyme
1/4 teaspoon white pepper
12 ounces clam juice
1½ cups milk

Make a paste of the flour and melted butter and set aside. Next sauté the shallots in the oil; add wine and seasonings and simmer to reduce wine for approximately three minutes. Stir in the clam juice and milk; add the flour paste and whip with a whisk until the sauce thickens. Strain before using.

BOEUF BOURGUIGNON

Serves Four

2 pounds lean stew beef
6 ounces lean salt pork
1 tablespoon cooking oil
2 tablespoons flour
2 cups red wine
2 cups beef stock
salt and pepper
1 sliced onion
1 bay leaf
1 celery branch
2 sliced carrots
4 mashed garlic cloves
1 whole clove
small pinch cinnamon
12 small cooked whole onions
1/2 pound fresh quartered mushrooms

Cut beef into 2-inch cubes and pork into ¼-inch by 1-inch strips. Sauté pork in oil over moderate heat until lightly browned, then remove to fireproof casserole. Sauté beef, several pieces at a time, in the hot oil and pork fat and add to casserole. Lightly sauté onion and carrots in the same fat. To meat mixture, add salt, pepper and enough flour to coat beef. Then add cooked carrots, sliced onions, bay leaf, celery, garlic, clove, cinnamon, wine and enough stock to cover meat. Bring to simmer on top of stove; cover casserole and place in lower part of oven preheated to 325°. Cook 2–3 hours or until a fork pierces the meat easily. When cooked, strain casserole over a sauce pan. Return the beef and pork to the casserole, adding the cooked whole onions and mushrooms that have been sautéed in butter. Skim fat off the strained sauce. If sauce is thick, add a small amount of beef stock. If sauce is thin, add a small amount of flour blended with melted butter. Add salt and pepper to taste. Pour sauce back into casserole over meat and vegetables. Cover and simmer a few minutes, basting meat and vegetables with the sauce several times. Serve from casserole or arrange on heated platter with potatoes, noodles or rice, garnished with parsley sprigs.

CHICKEN SUPREME EUGENE'S

Serves Two
2 chicken breasts
2 chicken legs
butter
flour
salt and pepper
8 fresh mushrooms
1/2 onion, finely sliced
1/2 teaspoon tarragon
1 cup dry sauterne
1 cup whipping cream
1/2 cup brown sauce
juice of 1/2 lemon

This dish is cooked entirely in the oven. Season the chicken with salt and pepper and dredge in flour. Pour enough melted butter in the bottom of a baking dish to amply cover, place chicken in dish and bake for 20 minutes at 300°, turning chicken, but not allowing it to brown. Add mushrooms and onion and cook five minutes longer. Sprinkle with tarragon, add sauterne, whipping cream, brown sauce and lemon juice and simmer until the liquid is reduced in half. Finish seasoning to taste. Eugene's recommends buttered boiled potatoes, rice or noodles to accompany the dish.

MEDALLION HELDER

Serves Four
1½ pounds fillet of beef (see below)
salt and pepper
flour
butter
1/2 cup madeira wine
1/2 cup brown sauce (see index)
truffles
3 large mushrooms, finely chopped
1/2 cup béarnaise sauce
4 teaspoons stewed tomatoes, chopped
4 thin slices french bread

Have your butcher insert a small strip of lard inside the fillet and divide them into four six-ounce portions. Sauté chopped mushrooms in a little butter with a truffle and blend in brown sauce; set aside. Roast the french bread in the oven until crisp. Prepare béarnaise sauce. Now to prepare the dish, season the fillets with salt and pepper and dredge lightly with flour. Sauté in butter to desired degree of rareness. Remove meat from skillet and drain off fat, leaving juice of beef. Add madeira wine and brown sauce with mushrooms and simmer until the liquid is reduced in half. Remove from fire; put meat back in the pan and coat with sauce. To serve, place each fillet on top of the toasted french bread; cover each with a tablespoon of béarnaise; place a teaspoon of stewed tomato in the center and top with a slice of truffle. Whip the remaining béarnaise sauce into the meat sauce and serve in a sauce dish with the fillet.

Carmel

POULET CHAUMIERE

Serves Four
2 spring chickens
salt and pepper
1 carrot, sliced
1 onion, sliced
thyme
1 bay leaf
6 tablespoons flour
1½ cups chablis wine
1½ cups chicken stock
6 tablespoons cooking oil
6 tablespoons heavy cream
butter
4 ounces truffles, sliced
3 ounces port wine
2/3 pound mushrooms, sliced

Bone, skin, and cut chicken in pieces; sprinkle with salt and pepper and sauté in oil. In another pan, sauté the sliced carrot and sliced onion in six tablespoons butter. When onion is slightly blond blend in flour. Add chicken stock and white wine and simmer 10 minutes. Strain sauce. Pour sauce over chicken; add thyme and bay leaves and simmer for about 30 minutes. Meanwhile sauté sliced mushrooms and truffles in butter. When chicken is cooked, add cream, port, mushrooms, and truffles and simmer in oven until ready to serve.

FROGMEAT CRÊPES WITH CURRY SAUCE

Serves Four
8 large frog legs
butter
8 6-inch French crêpes
1 cup white wine
juice of 1/2 lemon
1 pressed garlic pod
1 teaspoon curry powder
pinch powdered saffron
1 ounce Calvados
1½ cups curry sauce
tangerine slices
lemon slices
pumpkin seeds
lotus root slices

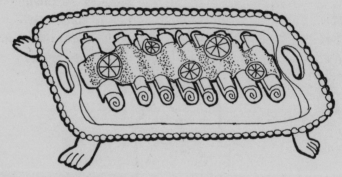

Bone out meat from frog legs. (You may substitute crab, chicken or lobster) Marinate for ten minutes in wine, lemon juice, and garlic. Sauté frogmeat briskly in butter, curry and saffron, and then enhance the sauce with Calvados. Fill crêpes with sauteed frogmeat; roll; cover with curry sauce and heat for a few minutes in oven. Garnish with tangerine, lemon, pumpkin seeds and lotus root.

CURRY SAUCE A LA RICHARD WING

Makes About 1½ Cups
1 slice minced Virginia Ham
1 ounce ground pork sausage
1 garlic clove, pressed
1 small onion, minced
8 mushrooms, minced
6 tablespoons butter
2 tablespoons flour
1/2 cup rich chicken stock
1/4 cup orange juice
1/4 cup white wine
1 cup fresh coconut milk
1 bay leaf
mace, nutmeg, paprika—dash
salt and pepper
1 teaspoon chopped parsley
dash tabasco sauce
2 teaspoons curry powder
1/2 cup cream
1 ounce of apple brandy

Sauté ham, sausage, garlic, onions, curry powder and mushrooms in 4 tablespoons butter. In another pan melt 2 tablespoons butter and blend in 2 tablespoons flour. Add chicken stock and stir constantly over low fire until thick and creamy. Add this sauce to the sauteed mixture; then add all other ingredients except cream and brandy, and simmer until sauce is reduced to half its volume. Correct seasoning and run through a sieve or blender. This may be prepared ahead of time. Before serving heat and at the last moment add cream and brandy. This sauce is also excellent with any fish, chicken or lamb dish.

ABALONE WITH CUCUMBER SOUBISE SAUCE

Serves Four
4 center cut abalone steaks
1 pound (approximately) clarified butter
2 cups chablis wine (approximately)
juice of one-half lemon
1 tablespoon peanut oil
nutmeg
salt and pepper
1—2 beaten eggs

Cucumber Soubise Sauce
2 tablespoons butter
2 tablespoons flour
1 cup fish stock (or clam juice)
2 tablespoons minced onions
1 small cucumber, peeled and chopped
tiny gherkins
tiny cocktail onions
1 teaspoon chopped chives
juice of one-half lemon
1 dash Angostura bitters
1 dash paprika
1 teaspoon horseradish
1 tablespoon dijon mustard
2 ounces chablis wine
1/4 cup pure cream
1 ounce cognac

Trim and pound steaks. Season with salt, pepper and nutmeg. Then marinate them in chablis and lemon juice for ten minutes and *no longer*. Strain away marinade. Dip abalone lightly in beaten eggs, then poach in very hot melted butter and peanut oil for *less than ten seconds*. Serve with cucumber soubise sauce and top each steak with a stuffed mushroom. Chef Richard Wing recommends one steak per person if this is to be served as a first course, two steaks per person for a main course.

Sauté minced onions in butter, blend in flour and add fish stock, stirring constantly until smooth and creamy. Add vegetables, seasoning and wine and cook for several minutes until well blended. Finish off with cream and cognac.

STUFFED MUSHROOMS IMPERIAL DYNASTY

8 large mushroom caps
8 small button mushrooms
1/2 pound minced raw seafood (a mixture
 of shrimps, lobster and sea bass or white fish)
1 tablespoon chopped chives
1 egg white
1 pinch mace
salt and pepper

Chef Richard Wing created these to serve with abalone, but they would also make excellent appetizers. First chop the seafood, being very careful not to chop too much as it will become rubbery. Add chives and seasoning to mixture and then bind with stiffly beaten egg whites. Stuff each cap with the filling and top with a button mushroom. Place in a covered steamer and cook fifteen minutes.

ESCARGOTS A LA IMPERIAL DYNASTY

Serves Four

24 imported French snails (canned)
1-1/3 cup butter
1 garlic clove
3 tablespoons chicken stock
2 tablespoons puree of cornish game hen, or
　(substitute strained veal or chicken baby food)
1 teaspoon dijon mustard
1½ tablespoons chopped shallots
2 teaspoons chopped parsley
dash tabasco or pepper
optional seasonings: grated fresh ginger,
　or dill weed, or ground clove, or nutmeg
　or cinnamon
1 ounce chablis wine
garlic salt
2 small white onions
1/4 cup fine breadcrumbs
sesame seeds (optional)
peanut oil
bicarbonate of soda (to wash shells)
french bread

The Wine and Food Society twice has awarded its Cordon Bleu for the Best Dish of the Year to Imperial Dynasty chef Richard Wing for his unique method of preparing escargots. A totally creative cook, Mr. Wing probably has never prepared the same dish in exactly the same way. Thus he suggests a number of optional seasonings above, with which you may experiment to your own taste.

Preparation of the shells:

Parboil shells in water to which the bicarbonate of soda has been added; rinse well and drain. Next deep fry shells in peanut oil; drain and sprinkle the inside of the shell with garlic salt. Then bake shells in oven.

Preparation of the snails

Dip the snails in boiling water for a few seconds and drain. Next pass them through hot peanut oil for a few seconds and drain. In a skillet sauté the mashed garlic clove and chopped shallots in butter until soft. Add meat puree, mustard, broth, parsley and snails; cook for a few minutes, but do not allow to boil. Add any of the suggested seasonings you wish very lightly to taste; add wine and cook for a few minutes longer. Stuff each shell with one snail, placing the soft part in the shell first; then fill the shell with the garlic sauce. Place on snail plate and sprinkle with fresh breadcrumbs, thinly sliced white onions and sesame seeds. When ready to serve, bake snails in hot oven (450°) until the sauce bubbles. Serve piping hot with french bread for dunking the sauce.

LOBSTER THERMIDOR

Serves Two
1 lobster 2—2½ pounds, cooked and split
flour
butter
pinch paprika
tabasco sauce
salt and pepper
whipping cream
1/2 cup chives
4 cups sliced mushrooms
1½ cups dry white wine
parmesan cheese
paprika

Have your butcher split and clean the lobster; and be sure to ask him to include the extra meat from the claws. Prepare a roux by blending 3 tablespoons flour into 3 tablespoons melted butter over low heat, stirring constantly; add cream and blend well; add paprika, tabasco, salt and pepper and stir until very thick and smooth; set aside. Remove the lobster meat from the shell and wash both the meat and the shell. Cut the meat into 1/2 inch pieces. Next sauté the chives in 4 tablespoons butter; add the mushrooms and cook together, stirring to assure that the mushrooms are completely coated with butter. Add the wine and simmer until reduced to one-third of volume. Add the butter and flour roux and stir until blended. Add the cooked lobster meat. Fill the half lobster shells with the lobster and sauce. The process up to now may be done ahead of time and refrigerated. When ready to serve, sprinkle the stuffed lobster with parmesan cheese, paprika and melted butter. Place in a pre-heated oven at 450° oven for 15 minutes.

BIBB LETTUCE VINAGRETTE

Serves Four
4 heads bibb or butter lettuce
2 hard boiled eggs, chopped
2 tablespoons shoestring beets
1/2 teaspoon chopped chives
vegetable or olive oil
wine vinegar
English dry mustard
salt and pepper

Remove outer leaves from lettuce heads and cut the
hearts in half. Wash, dry and chill. To serve, place
hearts only in salad bowl, and add chopped eggs,
beets and chives. Top with french dressing made in a
ratio of two parts oil to one part vinegar, adding
mustard, salt and pepper to taste.

FILET OF SOLE CHABLIS

Serves Four
4 large fillets of sole
1 cup chablis wine
1 tablespoon minced shallots
juice of 1/2 lemon
4 large mushroom caps
1 cup heavy cream
2 tablespoons flour
3 tablespoons butter

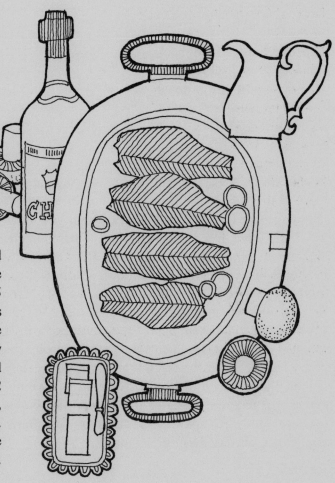

Melt one tablespoon butter in ovenproof skillet and sauté the shallots lightly. Remove from fire; place sole in pan; cover with wine and poach for 15 minutes on oven preheated to 350°. Remove fillets from pan and keep warm on a hot platter. Place cooking pan on top of stove and simmer over low heat until the wine is reduced in half. Add cream and lemon juice. In another pan blend flour into 2 tablespoons of melted butter and slowly add to sauce, stirring until the mixture is smooth and creamy. Simmer sauce for five minutes, then pour it over the sole and garnish each fillet with a mushroom cap. Serve very hot.

BEEF WELLINGTON

Serves Four
2—pound roast, filet of beef
4 ounces goose liver mousse
1/2 pound puff pastry dough
mushroom sauce (see index)
egg whites

If you are an expert at puff pastry, we suggest you make your own dough from your favorite recipe; if not, you may buy the puff pastry dough at French bakeries. Goose liver mousse may be purchased in jars or fresh at gourmet shops and delicatessans. Braise the roast in extremely hot pan until all sides of the meat are brown; refrigerate for 15 minutes. Mash the liver mousse, which should be quite moist; if not, add a little water to moisten. Spread the mousse on top of the filet to about 1/4 inch thickness. Roll out the pastry until 1/2-inch thick and roll completely around the roast; brush the pastry with egg whites. Cook roast in oven preheated to 350° for 25 minutes for rare meat, 35 minutes for medium rare. Serve with a rich, buttery mushroom sauce.

CHERRIES JUBILEE

Serves Four
3 ounces kirschwasser (kirsch and brandy)
4 scoops vanilla ice cream
32 pitted cherries with juice
1½ teaspoon fine sugar

In a chafing dish heat cherries, juice and sugar until boiling. Add kirschwasser and ignite, shaking pan gently until flame dies. Pour over ice cream and serve.

FILET OF BEEF DIANE DE L'AUBERGE

Serves Four
4 filet steaks, 7-ounce each
2 tablespoons olive oil
2 teaspoons shallots, finely chopped
juice of 1/2 lemon
1 teaspoon English mustard
dash worcestershire sauce
1 cup sour cream
1½ cups brown sauce (see index)
1 tablespoon chives, chopped
cognac
salt and pepper

Although many restaurants serve Steak Diane, it is not found in classic cookbooks, so each recipe is different. This version was created by George Bollag, owner-chef of L'Auberge, and is prepared there dramatically at the table by his partner, host Louis Frutschi. However, to do it at your dinner table, you must have a chafing dish with a very hot, adjustable flame. Otherwise, it is advisable to prepare it on your range. In either case, be sure you have all the ingredients, pre-measured at hand, as fast timing is the essence of its success. Have your butcher trim the steaks of all fat, butterfly them, and pound them flat to approximately 3/8-inch even thickness. Heat oil very hot, season meat with salt and pepper, and fry very quickly over hot flame until brown on each side. Add shallots, a jigger of cognac, flambé, remove meat and set aside. Lower flame. Add brown sauce, sour cream, worcestershire, mustard and lemon juice, stirring constantly with a fork or whisk until the sauce is bubbly. Add meat for a few seconds, then at the last moment the chives. Serve the steak at once, with the sauce poured over it.

PEACH FLAMBÉ TROCADERO

Serves Four
4 peeled peaches, quartered
1 teaspoon grated lemon rind
1 teaspoon grated orange rind
1 tablespoon sweet butter
2 tablespoons sugar
raspberry jelly or preserve
4 scoops vanilla ice cream
1 jigger cointreau
1 jigger cognac
1 jigger kirsch
1/2 cup toasted almonds, sliced

Again, the presentation of this dish is very important. If you are using fresh peaches, parboil them slightly; canned peaches when combined with this sauce are almost as delicious. Melt the butter in a chafing dish with sugar, orange and lemon rinds. Cook slowly until almost caramelized. Add peaches, 1 tablespoon raspberry jelly and cointreau. Warm fruit slowly in this sauce; meantime dish ice cream into bowls or sherbert glasses. Add the cognac and kirsch to the chafing dish and flambé. Top ice cream with the peaches and almonds; pour sauce over it while still flaming, and garnish with a dab of raspberry jelly. Serve immediately.

SALADE EXOTIQUE

Belgian endives
hearts of palm
avocado
watercress
hard boiled egg, grated
fresh chives, chopped

Dressing
1/4 cup lemon juice
salt and pepper
1/4 cup wine vinegar
1 teaspoon Dijon mustard
1 cup olive oil
1/2 teaspoon curry powder
3 teaspoons of Major Grey
  Chutney, chopped

Alternate on a very cold plate, slices of Belgian endive, avocado, heart of palm, and so on (all sliced lengthwise). Decorate with a sprig of watercress. Sprinkle with grated hard boiled egg and freshly chopped chives.

Blend first four ingredients. Add olive oil, curry powder and chutney. Mix well. Chill. Serve over salad.

VEAL KIDNEYS, FLAMED

Serves Four
4 milk-fed veal kidneys
1/4 cup armagnac (brandy)
clarified butter
dry marsala wine
1/4 teaspoon dry English mustard
2 teaspoons dijon mustard
3—4 dashes worcestershire sauce
freshly ground pepper
salt
3/4 cup duxelle of mushrooms (below)
1/2 cup veal or chicken stock
rice pilaf
4—6 tablespoons soft sweet butter

Cut the kidneys in 3/4 inch cubes. Sauté the cubes in very hot clarified butter for 3 to 4 minutes. Reduce the heat and put the kidney cubes on four skewers about 8 inches long. Slowly pour the cooking butter out of the pan, carefully retaining the kidney drippings in the pan. Place on high heat again and pour in armagnac. Ignite, shaking the pan until the fire burns out. Blend in mustard, worcestershire, salt and pepper. Next blend in mushroom duxelle, marsala and stock and simmer until smooth and medium thick. Lower heat and stir in soft butter until very smooth. Remove kidneys from skewers and mix well into sauce over low fire. Serve in a ring of rice pilaf.

Duxelle of Mushrooms
1 tablespoon white onions, chopped fine
1 tablespoon shallots, chopped fine
4 tablespoons butter
4 tablespoons oil
8—10 ounces white mushrooms
salt and pepper
1 tablespoon finely chopped pimientos
1/2 tablespoon chopped parsley

Chop mushrooms fine and then squeeze or press until almost completely free of juice. Chop shallots and onions together and sauté them in butter and oil for three minutes. Add pressed mushrooms and cook until the consistency of a paste. Add salt, pepper and pimientos. At the last minute mix in parsley.

ZUCCHINI AND RICE AU BOUILLON

Serves Eight
6 tablespoons butter
8 small zucchini, sliced 1/4 inch thick
1 large tomato, peeled and diced
2 cups cooked white rice
1 pint chicken consomme
salt and pepper
pinch rosemary

Melt butter in skillet on medium high heat. Add sliced zucchini (with skin) and sauté for one or two minutes. Add tomato, cooked rice, chicken broth and spices. Cover and cook slowly for 15 minutes. Zucchini should not be overcooked.

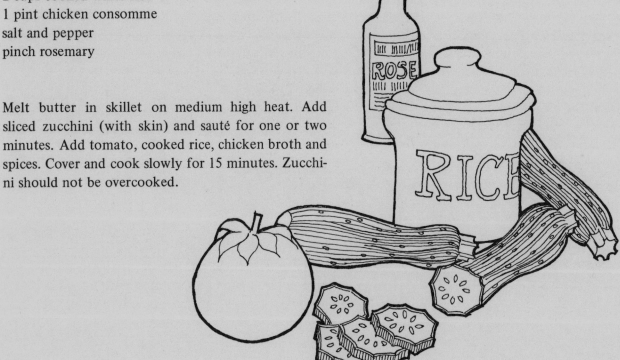

DOVER SOLE CHAMBERTIN

Serves Two to Three
1 pound filet of Dover sole
1 cup Chambertin (or any good red wine)
1/2 cup demi-glace (see index)
2 chopped shallots
5 ounces butter
1 tablespoon flour
pepper

Poach the sole gently with the shallots in wine which has been seasoned with a little pepper until the fish is cooked. Remove the sole and strain the sauce into another pan. Cook the wine sauce until reduced in half; add the demi-glace and bring to a boil. Blend together one tablespoon of the butter with the flour and blend into sauce. Bring to a boil again, remove from flame and stir in the rest of the butter. Arrange the sole on an oven-proof baking dish; cover with the sauce and glaze quickly in the broiler.

GOURMANDISE DE MIGNON DE VEAU

Serves Four
2 pounds veal loin, cut in thin scallops
8 french crêpes (see index)
butter
3/4 pound mushrooms, minced
1½ cups mornay sauce (see index)
flour, salt and pepper

Pound the scallops until very thin; sprinkle with salt and pepper and dust lightly with flour. Sauté the veal in melted butter on both sides until golden brown. Meanwhile, in another pan, sauté the minced mushrooms in butter; then spread them on the bottom of a ovenproof serving dish. Roll the veal in the crepes and place on top of the mushrooms; cover with mornay sauce and broil until golden.

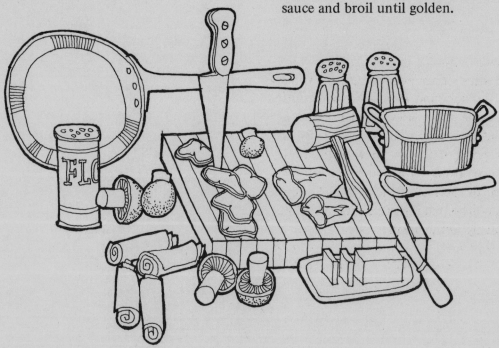

SOUFFLÉ GRAND MARNIER

Serves Two
1/2 cup milk
2 tablespoons sugar
pinch of salt
2 tablespoons sifted flour
4 ounces Grand Marnier
3 egg yolks
2 tablespoons butter
4 stiffly beaten egg whites

In a saucepan, bring milk to boil with sugar and salt. Blend flour with a little cold milk and add to heated milk. Add Grand Marnier and cook, stirring constantly for 2 or 3 minutes. Remove from fire and add egg yolks and butter. At the last moment, quickly fold in beaten egg whites and pour into a soufflé dish which has been buttered and sprinkled with fine sugar. Smooth the surface of the soufflé. Place soufflé on middle rack of pre-heated 400° oven; immediately reduce the temperature to 375° and bake 30 to 35 minutes. Two minutes before serving sprinkle with sugar to glaze.

CONSOMME BELLE VUE

Serves Six
2 cups clam broth
2 cups chicken broth
salt, white pepper
drop of tabasco
dash of sherry
1/2 pint whipping cream

Heat broth and season lightly. Fill consomme cups, top with whipped cream and glaze under broiler a few seconds.

LE SAUMON A LA VENITIENNE

1 medium sized salmon, skinned
2 branches celery, chopped
1/2 onion, chopped
1 carrot, chopped
dash vinegar
2 lemon slices
bay leaf
salt and pepper
2 sprigs parsley
white wine
sliced hard boiled eggs (garnish)
pimiento (garnish)
additional lemon for garnish

This is the creation of owner-chef Francois Sirgant. Allow about one-half pound of salmon per person. Sauté celery, onion and carrots in butter for about five minutes. Add 2 cups water, 2 cups wine and all other ingredients except the salmon and garnishes; bring to a boil. Place the salmon in the boiling vegetables so that they cover the salmon; cover pan and poach at just below simmer until salmon is cooked. Remove salmon from stock and cool; discard stock. To serve, coat the salmon with watercress sauce (below) and garnish with sliced eggs, lemons, pimientos and parsley. Chef Sirgant uses a very intricate method of slicing and garnishing the salmon, but for simplicity we suggest that you garnish it whole and serve it from the platter. Use your imagination with the garnish. The chef suggests cutting the lemon slices in a star shape; and making a design with the pimiento on top of the egg.

Watercress Sour Cream Sauce
1 pint sour cream
1 pint mayonnaise
1 bunch watercress, pureed
1 teaspoon anchovy paste
2 drops tabasco
finely chopped chives
green food coloring (optional)
white pepper
lemon juice

Combine sour cream, mayonnaise, watercress and anchovy paste and mix well. Correct seasoning with tabasco, lemon juice and white pepper. Fold in finely chopped chives to taste. The sauce should be pale green; if it is not, add a few drops of green food coloring.

ORANGE PETIT CHATEAU FLAMBÉ

Serves Four
6 sugar cubes
1 tablespoon orange marmalade
1 ounce kirsch
1 ounce cointreau or curacao
4 oranges, peeled and sectioned
French vanilla ice cream

120

In a chafing dish, melt sugar cubes until half carmelized, shaking the pan and stirring with a wooden spoon. Add orange marmalade and cook a bit longer. Add orange sections and cook several minutes longer. Add liqueurs and flame. The secret is to use real kirsch, not kirsch water. Serve each portion over three small scoops of vanilla ice cream.

GRENADIN DE VEAU GRAND DUFOUR

Serves Four
1½ pounds veal filet
Canadian bacon
American cheese
1/4 pound butter
2 cups fine bread crumbs
1—2 whole eggs, beaten
2 tablespoons salad oil
salt and pepper
paprika
flour
parsley
lemon juice

Sauce for Grenadin de Veau
4 slices Canadian bacon
salt, pepper and paprika
4 ounces cognac
2 cups consomme
4 tablespoons melted butter
1 cup pastry cream
juice of one lemon
2 egg yolks
2 ounces capers

The secret to this recipe is to slice the cheese and Canadian bacon paper thin. (Have your butcher do it or use a grater, but do not buy pre-sliced cheese and bacon as it is too thick.) Slice the veal into eight pieces and pound out to very thin slices about 6 by 4 inches. Sprinkle each veal slice with salt, pepper and paprika. Cover the center of each slice with the finely sliced cheese and bacon, leaving about one inch around the edge uncovered. Fold each slice in half, so that each piece is approximately 3 by 4 inches when folded. Dip each piece lightly in flour, then in egg, then in oil and finally in the breadcrumbs. Pound or pinch the edges gently to seal in the cheese. To cook, melt butter in large skillet over low fire and sauté breaded veal rolls ten minutes on each side, uncovered. Sprinkle with lemon juice while cooking. To serve, place veal on a platter, cover with the sauce, below, and garnish with lemon slices and parsley. Chef Paul Dufour suggests an accompaniement of risotto and creamed spinach.

Slice bacon into very narrow strips and sauté with salt, pepper and paprika. Add cognac and ignite, shaking pan until flame dies. Add consomme, melted butter and cook for ten minutes. Reduce heat so that mixture is not boiling and add cream, lemon juice, egg yolks and capers, stirring constantly until sauce is creamy and smooth.

OYSTERS AU CHAMPAGNE

Serves Four as Appetizer
24 medium-size oysters in shells
1 cup non-sparkling champagne or dry white wine
juice of one lemon
salt and pepper
3 tablespoons butter
3 tablespoons flour
1/2 cup pastry cream
1/4 cup grated parmesan cheese

Remove oysters from shells; reserve the largest half of each shell and scrub it well. Poach the oysters in wine for five minutes at a temperature just below the boiling point. Add salt and pepper to taste and lemon juice. Place one oyster on each of the scrubbed shells, and retain wine in which they have been cooked. In another pan melt butter slowly and blend in flour. Whisk until smooth and slowly blend in cream over low heat stirring constantly until smooth and thick. Add cream sauce and grated cheese to the poaching wine and stir over low heat until thick. Cover the oysters with the sauce and bake at 350° for ten minutes.

CRÊPES SUZETTE

8 crêpes   (see index)
1/4 pound sweet butter
1 tablespoon sugar
juice of 1/2 orange
lemon rind
orange rind
1 ounce grand marnier
1 ounce cointreau
2 ounces cognac

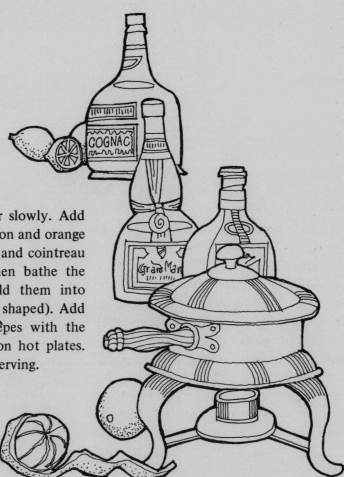

In a chafing dish pan, melt the butter slowly. Add sugar, orange juice and grate a little lemon and orange rind into the sauce. Add grand marnier and cointreau and stir until sauce well blended. Then bathe the pancakes in the hot nectar and fold them into quarters (so that they are triangularly shaped). Add the cognac and ignite. Baste the crêpes with the flaming sauce and serve immediately on hot plates. Pour the sauce from the pan over each serving.

OMELETTE NORVEGIENNE

Serves Eight
10–12 egg whites
1 quart Neapolitan ice cream
(or other flavor if desired)
3–4 ounces sponge cake
rum
1/2 cup sugar

Chef Gregoire, executive chef at L'Escoffier Restaurant in the Beverly Hilton Hotel, is also a noted teacher of French cuisine at his Le Gourmet French Cooking School. Following are two of his recipes. Chef Gregoire advises that this dessert, better known as a baked alaska, may be made in advance and kept in the freezer until ready to serve. Place the sponge cake on a platter, preferably oval shaped, and sprinkle with rum. Spread the ice cream on the cake and keep in freezer. Beat egg whites until almost stiff; add sugar and beat until stiff. Place one-third of the egg whites in a pastry bag with a fancy tube for decoration. Spread the remaining egg whites over the ice cream with a spatula, then decorate the baked alaska with the egg whites in pastry bag. Place in 500° oven for several minutes until brown and serve.

ROAST PORK WITH MILK

Serves Six
2 quarts certified milk
center cut loin of pork
garlic cloves
salt and pepper
oil or fat
1 onion, chopped
1 small bay leaf
1/2 teaspoon rosemary
1/2 teaspoon thyme
2 tablespoon melted butter
2–3 tablespoons flour
brandy (optional)
chopped parsley

For the preparation of this pork dish, Chef Gregoire advises using certified milk only, which is available at health food stores. Have your butcher remove the back bones and trim the fat from the loin of pork. (The fat may be saved to use in pâté.) Cut back around the rib bones about an inch before cooking so that paper frills may be placed on the ribs to decorate the roast for serving. Make several slits in the meat and insert garlic cloves; then season roast with salt and pepper. Brown roast in fat or oil, starting with the fat side down. In another pan, sauté the onion, thyme, bay leaf and rosemary. To cook the roast use a deep roasting pan about the same size as the roast (a larger pan will use too much milk). Place the onion mixture in the bottom of the pan and place the roast on top of the onions. In a saucepan bring the milk to a boil with a little salt and pour it over the meat until the roast is covered. Bring the milk to a boil again on top of the stove; and cook, uncovered, at 375° in the oven for at least 1 hour, without moving in order not to break the crust. Then turn the meat over and cook another 1/2 hour or until done. When meat is cooked, remove from pan; strain the sauce and simmer until it is reduced to 2 or 3 cups. Combine the flour and melted butter, and add a little at a time to the sauce, stirring constantly until the sauce is smooth and thick. Strain the sauce again, and add a little brandy if desired and chopped parsley. Decorate the roast with paper frills and serve with the sauce.

125

QUICHE LORRAINE

Serves Six to Eight as Appetizer
For the Dough
1 cup flour
5 tablespoons butter, softened
pinch of salt
1 egg
1–1½ tablespoons milk

Beat the egg very lightly. Make a crown of the flour and put into it 1½ tablespoons of the beaten egg, salt and butter. Add a little of the milk and mix thoroughly, but lightly for as short a time as possible. If dough is too dry add milk until it is moist but not sticky. Roll dough flat and line one 9-inch pie tin.

For the Filling
2 slices bacon, diced
2 ounces (or more) diced Swiss cheese
1 pint half-and-half
4 eggs, lightly beaten
butter
one small onion, very finely chopped
  (optional)
1/2 teaspoon salt
2 pinches pepper
2 pinches nutmeg

Boil and drain the bacon. Sauté the onion in butter for a few minutes, until tender but not yellow. Remove pan from heat and add the half-and-half and the eggs to the onion. Season with salt, pepper and nutmeg. Place the bacon and cheese in the bottom of the lined pie pan and then pour in the egg and half-and-half batter. Bake 30 to 35 minutes in a moderate oven (350°–400°) until lightly browned on top and the custard is set. The amount of cheese can be increased greatly to taste.

CARRE DE PORC A L'ORANGERIE

Serves Eight
6-pound rack of pork
2 oranges
powdered sugar
1 tablespoon sugar
1 tablespoon granulated sugar
1 teaspoon vinegar
1 pint orange juice
1 pint condensed beef bouillon
2 tablespoons butter
1 tablespoon cognac
salt and pepper

Season pork rack with salt and freshly ground black pepper. Wrap in aluminum foil, place in roaster and cook at 400° for two hours. Remove foil; garnish top of rack with orange sections and sprinkle with powdered sugar. Heat oven to highest temperature and cook pork another ten minutes or until it is golden brown. Serve with orange and cognac sauce.

To make the sauce
Brown granulated sugar with a little water in a heavy pan. Add vinegar and orange juice and simmer for ten minutes. Add bouillion and cook until the sauce is reduced in half. Strain the sauce; whip in melted butter; add cognac, blending well.

LA CROQUETTE DE CREVETTE

Serves Four
1/4 pound butter
finely chopped shallots
1/2 cup flour
1 tablespoon tomato paste
3 cups milk
3 mushrooms, finely chopped
1/2 pound tiny shrimp, cooked
salt and pepper to taste
pinch cayenne
flour
1–2 eggs, beaten
fine bread crumbs
vegetable oil
chopped parsley

La Croquette de Crevette is a specialty from the Belgian coast between France and Holland, rarely served or known outside that area. Lucien Brack, owner-chef of the Old Brussels, has introduced the dish to Californians, as an occasional specialty on his menu. To make the croquettes, melt the butter and lightly cook the shallots. Add the flour, stirring constantly with a whisk until well blended. Blend in tomato paste; then blend in milk; stir until thickened; and continue to cook over very low heat (or over water) until it is the consistency of a *very* thick cream sauce. Add chopped mushrooms and bay shrimp and mix well. Add salt, pepper and cayenne and refrigerate for 2 to 3 hours. When ready to serve, form the shrimp mixture into balls or oblong shapes; roll in flour; dip in beaten eggs; roll well in bread crumbs; and deep fry at high heat for 2 to 4 minutes. Serve with chopped parsley.

CARBONADE FLAMANDE

Serves Four
1½ pounds finely sliced beef sirloin
flour, salt and pepper
2 onions, thinly sliced
beer
dash worcestershire sauce
1 tablespoon fine sugar
butter or vegetable oil

This is an original dish of Belgium, rarely found in America. It is served as a specialty at Old Brussels from time to time. Lightly flour the beef and season with salt and pepper. Sauté in butter or oil over high flame. In another pan, sauté the onions in butter until very brown; then add to beef. Cover the onion and beef mixture with beer; reduce heat; add a dash of worcestershire; cover and simmer for 45 minutes. Before serving add sugar, more or less to taste. Serve with boiled potatoes.

STEAMED CLAMS MARINIÉRE

Serves Two to Four
24 clams in shells
butter
pinch of crushed garlic
1 teaspoon minced shallots
1 pinch crushed bay leaf
1 pinch cayenne
1 cup white wine
freshly ground pepper
2 tablespoons butter
2 tablespoons flour
1 cup clam juice
lemon juice
chopped parsley

First make a thick cream sauce: blend the flour into two tablespoon melted butter and slowly stir in the clam juice. Cook over very low heat or hot water while you are preparing the clams. Scrub clams well to remove all dirt and sand from the shells. Then sauté the garlic, shallots, and bay leaf in enough melted butter to amply cover the bottom of a heavy pot. Add the cayenne and place the clams in the pot. Add white wine and season with pepper. Cover the pot securely and steam until the clams open (about 15 minutes.) Remove the clams to a platter and keep warm. Finish the sauce by adding the cream sauce to the liquid in the pot; add a squeeze of fresh lemon juice; and stir until sauce is well blended and creamy. Pour the sauce over the clams and sprinkle with chopped parsley.

CHICKEN SUZANNE

Serves Four
4 whole chicken breasts, boned and skinned
salt and white pepper
cayenne
paprika
MSG
flour
butter
1/2 cup white wine
12 melon balls
1—16-ounce can plums
2 tablespoons butter
2 tablespoons brown sugar
juice of ½ lemon
pinch cinnamon
1/2 teaspoon vanilla extract
2 teaspoons cornstarch
1 cup dry sherry
shredded coconut

Method for Plum Sauce
Remove pits from plums and mash, retaining juice. In a saucepan blend brown sugar into melted butter and add sherry. Blend in plums and juice; season with vanilla extract, cinnamon and lemon juice. Cook over low fire until mixture begins to simmer. Then thicken with cornstarch blended with a little water.

Method for Chicken
Season chicken with salt, pepper, cayenne, paprika and MSG. Flour both sides lightly, brown in butter, add wine and simmer for approximately five minutes. Meanwhile, heat melon balls in water in a separate pan. When chicken is cooked, add plum sauce and simmer long enough for chicken to absorb fragrance of the sauce. Serve over rice, sprinkle with shredded coconut and garnish with melon balls.

SWEETBREADS A LA SERGE

Serves Four
2 pounds sweetbreads
1/2 onion, chopped
1 carrot, chopped
1 celery branch, chopped
1 bay leaf
10 peppercorns
1 leek, sliced
1 pinch thyme
salt
3 quarts water

This first part of the recipe may be made the previous day, advises Ondine chef Alfred Roblin. Soak the sweetbreads in cool water for six hours. Then slowly boil all the other ingredients above for 15 minutes; add the sweetbreads and simmer for 30 minutes. Let them cool in the stock.

To Finish The Dish
2 whole eggs, beaten
2 tablespoons dry sherry
2 medium-thick slices ham
2 artichoke bottoms, cooked or canned
4 tablespoons butter
lemon juice
fine white bread crumbs
chopped parsley (garnish)
salt, pepper and flour

Cut artichoke bottoms and ham in narrow strips and set aside. Cut sweetbreads in half lengthwise; sprinkle with salt and pepper; dip in flour, then in egg, then in breadcrumbs. Place sweetbreads in a pan with 2 tablespoons butter and cook slowly on both sides until golden brown. While sweetbreads are cooking, place the artichokes, ham and sherry in a small pan and cook slowly until the sherry has evaporated. Place the cooked sweetbreads on a hot serving dish; place the artichokes and ham on top; and sprinkle lightly with lemon juice. Quickly brown 2 tablespoons of butter; pour over the completed dish; sprinkle with parsley and serve.

PHEASANT ONDINE

Serves Four
To Make the Stock and Veloute
2 pheasants (2½ pounds each) dressed
1 onion, chopped fine
1 carrot, chopped fine
1 branch celery, chopped fine
1 leek, chopped fine
1 bay leaf
1 pinch thyme
4 cloves juniper
4 tablespoons dry sherry
4 cups water   6 tablespoons butter
salt and pepper   6 tablespoons flour

Disjoint the bird, breaking the leg at the thigh joint. Reserve the breast and thigh and cut up the carcass and leg bone into small pieces for the stock. Place the stock bones in a saucepan with the sherry; cover and simmer until the sherry is evaporated. Add the vegetables, seasonings and water; bring to boil; reduce heat and simmer for 1½ hours. To make the veloute, melt the butter in a sauce pan, add the flour and blend with a whisk. Add two cups of the pheasant stock; bring to a boil; reduce heat and cook for ten minutes.

To cook the pheasant and finish sauce
1/4 pound butter
1 ounce vodka
8 sliced mushroom caps
4 chopped shallots
1 pint sour cream
salt, pepper and MSG

Melt butter in large skillet; add pheasant breasts and thighs; cover and cook slowly for 30 minutes, turning once or twice without allowing to brown. "The color of the bird *must* remain pale," warns Ondine chef Alfred Roblin. Remove the bird and place on hot serving dish. Using the same skillet sauté the mushrooms, *fast*. Add the vodka and when this is almost reduced add the shallots and cook quickly, but do not allow to brown. Add 3/4 cup of the veloute, and stirring slowly with a whisk, bring to a boil. Remove from the fire and add the sour cream. Put back on fire just long enough to warm the sour cream. Season to taste; pour over the bird and serve.

BOUILLABAISSE

Serves Four
1/3 cup sliced onions
1/3 cup sliced leeks
1/3 cup sliced celery
1 bay leaf
1 pinch thyme or fennel
2 garlic cloves, mashed
2 tablespoons olive oil
1/2 cup clam juice
1/2 cup sauterne wine
1/4 gram (1 small pinch) pure saffron
1/2 cup peeled and diced tomatoes
1½ pounds mixed white fish (rock cod, etc.)
shrimp and/or crab (optional)
cornstarch
garlic croutons

Slice vegetables julienne style (thin strips lengthwise) and sauté them in olive oil until tender. Add garlic, bay leaf, thyme, clam juice, wine and tomatoes and simmer slowly for about 20 minutes. Thicken slightly with a little cornstarch mixed with water and add saffron. Remove bones from one or more kinds of white fish, depending on what is available fresh, and cut into chunks. Place fish in individual baking dishes or ovenproof casserole; pour soup mixture over the fish and bake at 400° for about ten minutes, or until fish is flaky. You may add precooked shellfish at the last moment, or raw shellfish several minutes before the whitefish is cooked. Serve in the baking dishes or from the casserole with garlic croutons.

BRAISED OXTAILS JARDINIERE

Serves Four

4 pounds sectioned oxtails
1 large onion, roughly chopped
2 carrots, cut up
1 celery rib, sliced
1 bay leaf
1 pinch whole thyme
2 garlic cloves, minced
salt and pepper
1 cup burgundy
6 tablespoons tomato sauce
cooking oil
1 cup pearl onions (for garnish)
1 cup small carrots (for garnish)
1 cup green peas (for garnish)
cornstarch

In a dutch oven, brown oxtails with vegetables and spices. Add wine, tomato sauce and enough water to cover the meat, and simmer for 3 to 4 hours or until tender. Remove oxtails to hot serving platter; skim fat from stock in which they were cooked and thicken stock with cornstarch dissolved in water. Garnish oxtails with cooked pearl onions, small carrots and peas and serve with sauce.

CREAM OF WATERCRESS SOUP

Serves Six
butter
1 onion, chopped fine
1 leek, chopped fine
2 celery branches, chopped fine
2 bunches watercress
2 carrots
2 pounds diced potatoes
salt and white pepper
bay leaf
pinch thyme
chicken broth
heavy cream

Sauté onion, leek and celery in clarified butter until lightly golden. Add watercress, carrots, potatoes and seasonings. Add chicken stock until the stock is one inch over the top of the vegetables. Cover and simmer for one hour. Then puree by running through a blender. Return mixture to pan and bring to a boil. Before serving, add butter and heavy cream to taste. Sprinkle a few leaves of watercress on each serving.

TARTARE STEAK

Serves one as main course
10 ounces lean raw top sirloin
2 anchovy fillets
1 teaspoon dijon mustard
1 dash Tabasco
1/2 teaspoon worcestershire sauce
1 dash dry sherry
1 dash wine vinegar
1 dash vegetable oil
1 egg yolk
salt and pepper to taste
chopped parsley
chopped onions
capers
1 hard boiled egg, chopped
extra thin rye toast

The Riviera serves Steak Tartare as a main course. We have found that the portion below, for one, makes an extraordinary hors d'oeuvre. Have your butcher grind once only, using large grind, the top sirloin. The cut here is the secret as filet mignon becomes too mushy and other cuts are too tough or fatty. In a wooden bowl, smash anchovies and add mustard, tabasco, worcestershire, sherry, vinegar, egg yolk and salt and pepper to taste. Add raw meat and mix well. Then add several teaspoons of parsley, onions and capers to your taste; add chopped egg; mix well again and chill. If this is to be served as a main course, rebuild the mixture on a serving plate like two small filet mignons and serve uncooked with rye toast. If this is to be served as an hors d'oeuvre, build the mixture into one attractively shaped mound on a platter; garnish with parsley and circle with rye toast. (Note: It tastes even better if refrigerated overnight.)

137

VEAL CORDON BLEU

Serves Four
8 4-ounce veal scallops
8 very thin slices Swiss cheese
8 very thin slices ham
flour
salt and pepper
l egg
fine bread crumbs
grated parmesan cheese
butter
1/2 cup milk
1/2 cup veal or chicken stock

Flatten scallops until 1/4 inch thick. Sprinkle with salt and pepper. Place a slice of cheese and a slice of ham on each scallop. Roll up scallops and tie with string. Dust scallops with flour, dip in beaten egg and roll in bread crumbs. Then sauté in clarified butter over medium heat until golden brown. Meanwhile make a veal velouté by melting 2 tablespoons butter over low heat. Blend in 2 tablespoons flour. Add milk and veal stock and stir until thick and creamy. Season with salt and pepper to taste. Spread two tablespoons of the veal velouté on each rolled scallop, sprinkle with parmesan and glaze under broiler. Before serving pour around each cutlet a ring of Madeira sauce with mushrooms.

Madeira Sauce with Mushrooms
1 cup sliced fresh mushrooms
1/3 cup Madeira wine
2 tablespoons butter
2 tablespoons flour
2 cups beef stock
salt and pepper

Sauté mushrooms in butter. Blend in flour and slowly add beef stock. Cook until thickened, stirring constantly. Add Madeira, salt and pepper to taste and simmer for 5 minutes.

TOURNEDOS OF BEEF QUEEN OF SHEBA

Serves Four
8 medallions defatted tenderloin
1 large eggplant
1/4 pound prosciutto ham, sliced thin
8 large mushroom caps
lemon juice
1 jigger white wine
16 jumbo asparagus tips
flour
butter
salt and pepper

Peel eggplant and cut into 1/2 inch slices; dust lightly with flour and sauté in butter until golden brown. In another pan, sauté the mushroom in butter with white wine and a dash of lemon juice. Warm prosciutto ham in the oven. Season beef with salt and pepper and dust lightly with flour; then sauté to desired degree of rareness. To serve, place a slice of the eggplant on the dish, cover with prosciutto, place beef on top, cover with sauce (below) and cap with a mushroom. Pyramid the asparagus tips on the sides.

Sauce for Tournedos of Beef
1 tablespoon finely chopped shallots
1/2 cup brown sauce   (see index)
1 ounce red burgundy wine
butter

Sauté the shallots in butter for one minute. Add brown sauce; bring to simmer and add burgundy.

BLACK CHERRY SOUP

Serves Six
butter
1 tablespoon flour
2 cups warm water
2 pounds stoned black cherries
1 pinch sugar
few drops of kirsch
French bread

Melt one tablespoon of butter in saucepan. Add a tablespoon of flour, and stir well, not allowing it to color. Add the warm water, cherries, sugar, and kirsch. Let simmer until cherries are cooked. Pour mixture, still bubbling, over slices of French bread, fried in butter, in a soup tureen. Serve as hot as possible.

ESCALOPINES DE VEAU AUX CEPES
Veal Scallops with Mushrooms

Serves Four
12 1½ ounce slices leg of white veal
salt and pepper
flour
6 tablespoons sweet butter
chopped fresh shallots
finely chopped French cepes
   (or mushrooms)
1/2 glass dry white wine
freshly chopped parsley

Pound veal very thin, season with salt and pepper and dip lightly in flour. Melt butter in thick frying pan. When very hot, add veal and brown on both sides for six minutes. Remove scallops; add chopped shallots and mushrooms and sauté for two minutes. Add wine and bring to a quick boil. Return scallops to pan and cook for two minutes. Place scallops on a heated platter; pour sauce over meat; sprinkle with parsley and serve.

The restaurants on the following pages best exemplify the composite California cuisine. They have taken the foods of many countries and adapted them to their own way of cooking. Sam's Grill, one of San Francisco's oldest restaurants, was one of the first to set an international table, combining their own methods of preparing seafood, with French and Italian dishes, California specialties like Hangtown Fry, and all-American favorites such as Coney Island Clam Chowder. In recent years, the California-International kitchen has been carried to the ultimate degree by restaurateurs like "Trader Vic" Bergeron, who runs two distinct kitchens, Oriental and Continental, in one locale (we have included his recipes in the Far East section of this book). At two newer restaurants, King's Four in Hand and the Imperial Dynasty (see section on French cooking), Chinese and French seasonings and ingredients are often combined in the same dish. The message of these restaurateurs is clear: be creative, experiment and combine the best of all cuisines.

JINNY SMEDSRUD'S FAMOUS OATMEAL BREAD

Two loaves
2 cups boiling water
1 cup Old Fashioned Quaker Oats
1/2 cup molasses
1 tablespoon butter
1 package active compressed yeast
1/2 cup warm water
6 cups all purpose flour, sifted
2 teaspoons salt

Pour the boiling water over the rolled oats, salt, and butter. Stir rapidly and let stand one hour. Add yeast, which has been softened in warm water, then the molasses and flour. Beat until well mixed. Let rise in a warm place, away from drafts, until double in size. Beat the second time until smooth as possible. Pour into two greased 9x5x3 inch pans and let rise until double in bulk. Bake in a 350° oven, for 1 hour, or until bread starts to pull away from sides of pan. Cool before slicing.

OYSTER SOUP

Makes About Eight Cups
1½ branches celery, chopped
1/2 medium onion, chopped
1 pint oysters
1 quart water
1 tablespoon salt
1 small garlic clove, crushed
1/4 teaspoon white pepper
1 bay leaf
1 medium potato, diced
2 tablespoons clam juice
2 cups milk
butter
chopped leaves of the celery

Sauté the celery and onion in butter for ten minutes. Add oysters cut into preferred size and all other ingredients except milk. Bring to a boil and simmer for about 20 minutes or until the potatoes are cooked. If a thicker soup is desired, add some flour and water paste. Add milk; heat but do not boil and serve.

GREEK LEMON SOUP

Serves Eight
2 quarts chicken-rice soup
1/4 pound butter
1 teaspoon powdered chicken stock
1/2 cup sauterne
3 egg yolks
juice of two lemons
finely chopped parsley

Prepare chicken-rice soup according to your favorite recipe or substitute canned soup. Add butter, chicken stock and wine and simmer gently for 20 to 30 minutes. In a separate bowl, beat egg yolks and lemon juice until frothy. When ready to serve, whisk 1 cup of the hot soup into the egg-lemon mixture, then pour all back into the soup kettle. Serve immediately garnished with thin slices of lemon or finely chopped parsley. By adding extra rice, as the Greeks do, this makes a fine one-course meal.

BREAST OF CHICKEN DEL SUR

Serves Eight
2 cans cream of mushroom soup
1/4 cup sherry
1 cup sour cream
1/2 teaspoon salt
1/8 teaspoon pepper
1/8 teaspoon garlic powder
8 whole chicken breasts
sauterne
16 thinly sliced large mushroom caps
butter
paprika

Have your butcher halve, bone and skin the chicken breasts. In a large pot with a tight fitting lid, simmer breasts in 1/2 inch of sauterne for one hour. Drain breasts and brown lightly in butter in a hot frying pan. Meanwhile make the sauce by heating mushroom soup, sherry, sour cream, salt, pepper and garlic powder. Arrange the breasts in a shallow casserole or 8 individual baking dishes. Pour the sauce over the chicken, top with sliced mushrooms, dot with butter and dust lightly with paprika. A few minutes before serving, place under high broiler until bubbling and lightly browned.

147

COCK-A-LEEKIE SOUP

Serves Eight
1½ bunches leeks
2 pounds potatoes, diced
2 onions, diced
6 branches celery, diced
salt and pepper to taste
4 cups chicken stock or base
half-and-half (to finish)
1/4 pound butter

Sauté diced vegetables in butter until soft. Add chicken stock and diced potatoes, and simmer for 1½ hours. Whip or run through a blender. Before serving, reheat mixture to boiling point and add half-and-half until consistency of a thick cream soup. Salt and pepper to taste.

CORNISH PASTIES

Makes Six Pasties
3/4 pound bottom round steak
3/4 pound diced onions, potatoes,
   turnips
2 ounces fine ground beef suet
salt and pepper
1 pound short crust pastry
egg wash for pastry

Chop bottom round steak in very fine dice. Mix together vegetables and diced meat, salt, pepper and suet. Roll out pastry and cut out six circles (about the size of a saucer) with the lid of a pan. Brush with egg white around the edges. Then put the meat and vegetable mixture in half of the circle; fold the other half of pastry over the filling; and pinch the edges with your fingers. Place on baking tray in a moderate oven (350°) for about one hour. Serve hot. By using a smaller circle, these make excellent hors d'oeuvres.

LANCASHIRE HOT POT

Serves Four to Five
2½ pounds lamb neck
2 large onions
4 medium potatoes
4 carrots
1/2 pound mushrooms
1½ pints beef stock
1 dozen oysters (optional)
salt and pepper
butter
chopped parsley

This is chef Malcolm Stroud's version of the classic Lancashire miner's dinner. Have your butcher cut the lamb neck into chops of sufficient thickness to make two layers in the dutch oven or casserole in which you will be cooking this dish. Slice vegetables. Place a layer of vegetables (except potatoes) in the bottom of the casserole; cover with a layer of lamb chops; add another layer of vegetables, another layer of meat, another layer of vegetables, and finally the potatoes on top. Season each layer lightly with salt and pepper as you build the casserole. Pour beef stock over casserole and dot the potatoes with butter. Place casserole uncovered in a 400° oven until the potatoes are lightly browned. Then reduce the heat to 300°, cover the casserole and cook for about three hours. Garnish with parsley and serve from the pot.

FRUIT TRIFLE

Serves Eight
1 large jam sponge roll
  (strawberry or rasberry)
1/2 pint English custard (see below)
1½ pounds fresh fruit (see below)
1/2 pint whipping cream, whipped
1 cup cream sherry
1/4 cup brandy
12 fresh strawberries

Malcom Stroud of The Coachman recommends Bird's brand of English custard. For the fruit you may use any combination of peaches, strawberries, rasberries, bananas, pineapples, cherries, apricots, etc., peeled and sliced. To prepare the dessert, slice the jam sponge roll and lay the slices in the bottom of a large dessert bowl. Place the fruit on top of the sponge roll; pour on the sherry and brandy and allow to soak well through the fruit. Add the heated custard and chill. Before serving, cover the top with whipped cream and arrange a dozen fresh strawberries on top for garnish

SPLIT PEA SOUP

Makes About Eight Cups
3 cups dried peas, washed
1 large onion, chopped
2 cups carrots, diced
meat from 2 smoked ham hocks, diced
1 large potato, diced
salt
pepper
1 clove garlic, pressed
2 bay leaves, whole
1 tablespoon Indian curry
sour cream

Wash the dried peas and cover with water to 1 inch over the top. Bring to simmer, occasionally stirring so peas don't burn. Cook until peas are soft like a thick puree. Add all other ingredients except sour cream. Transfer to a double boiler and simmer slowly for 4 hours. Soup may be served as is or run through a blender. Serve with a dab of sour cream.

BEEF STROGANOFF

Serves Four
1/2 pound large mushrooms, sliced
2 onions, sliced thin
1 pound bald tip (or round steak)
1 teaspoon salt
1/2 teaspoon pepper
1 teaspoon sweet basil
1 garlic clove, pressed
1¼ cups sherry
1 pint sour cream
safflower oil

This is Richard Dehr's variation of the classic Russian dish. Cut meat into 1/2 x 6 inch strips. Put in mixing bowl. Mix meat and seasonings; add enough oil to moisten and knead by hand. Sauté onions and mushrooms in safflower oil. Braise meat. Mix meat with onions and mushrooms in dutch oven. Cover with sherry and bring to a boil. Cook at low temperature until the alcoholic smell of the sherry has gone, about 1 hour. Add sour cream and cook until the sour cream has a brownish color.

BEEF RISOTTO

Serves Six
butter
olive oil
1 pound ground sirloin
salt
pepper
garlic
1/2 cup sherry
6 jumbo stuffed olives with pimiento, sliced
1/2 green pepper, diced
1 small onion, diced
1 fresh tomato, diced
2 tablespoons parmesan cheese
2/3 cup tomato sauce
1 cup cooked rice
slices of mild cheddar cheese

This is Richard Dehr's own version of Risotto. Sauté onion and green pepper in oil; then add tomatoes and olives and cook for a few minutes. In another pan, preferably an 8-inch skillet, put just enough butter and olive oil to cover pan, and braise meat seasoned with salt, pepper and garlic. Add vegetables, tomato sauce, cooked rice, sherry, and parmesan. Simmer a few minutes to reduce sherry. Cover with slices of cheddar. On top of the cheese make a cross with the left over tomato sauce. Cover and simmer over a low fire for 15 minutes.

MARJORIE DEHR'S ROLLS

Makes Sixteen Rolls
1 tablespoon butter
2 tablespoons honey
3/4 cup milk
1 tablespoon dry activated yeast
2 cups stone ground whole wheat flour
1 cup pastry whole wheat flour
1/2 teaspoon salt

Dissolve butter, honey and salt in 1/4 cup hot water over low fire. Add milk and heat until luke warm. Dissolve yeast in 1/4 cup lukewarm water and add to honey and milk mixture. Combine the two flours and stir enough flour into liquid mixture until thick enough to knead. Knead until stiff and plastic, thick and heavy; then let dough rise until twice the original size. When risen, divide dough into two parts and roll out each part until the size of a thick pie curst. Cut each part into eight wedges, and roll each wedge from the wide end to the narrow to form the rolls. Allow to rise again until twice the size. Bake at 450° in lightly oiled pan for about 12 minutes.

CREAM OF ABALONE SOUP

Makes Approximately Eight Cups
1 pound ground abalone
1 cup chopped onions
1 cup chopped celery
1 cup diced potatoes
1 quart hot milk
1 cup clam juice
1 teaspoon MSG
2 tablespoons flour
1/4 cup butter
salt and pepper to taste
dash of worcestershire sauce
dash of tabasco

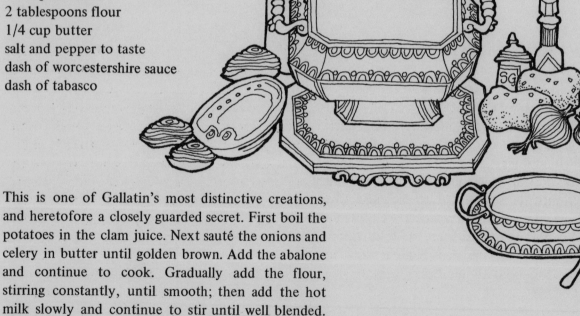

This is one of Gallatin's most distinctive creations, and heretofore a closely guarded secret. First boil the potatoes in the clam juice. Next sauté the onions and celery in butter until golden brown. Add the abalone and continue to cook. Gradually add the flour, stirring constantly, until smooth; then add the hot milk slowly and continue to stir until well blended. Finally add the boiled potatoes. Season to taste with MSG, salt, pepper, worcestershire, tabasco and clam juice.

STEAK JEHANNE

Serves Six
6 filet mignon steaks
1/2 pound thinly sliced mushrooms
butter
1/2 cup finely sliced onions
1½ cups beef stock
dry red wine
2 teaspoons flour
salt, pepper, paprika
6 large, cooked mushroom caps
1 jigger cognac

To Make the Sauce

Sauté sliced mushrooms in butter until tender; add 1/2 cup of the beef stock and simmer for ten minutes. In another pan, sauté onions in butter until tender; then add 1 cup of the beef stock and 1/2 cup of wine. Blend in flour; add sauteed mushroom slices; and season with salt, pepper and paprika.

To Prepare the Meat

Butterfly steaks by slicing almost all the way through the center; then open up into a butterfly shape; cover with wax paper and pound lightly with a meat cleaver for uniform thickness. Marinate the steaks and the cooked mushroom caps in the sauce for about ten minutes. To finish the dish, sauté the steaks in butter to which a little of the sauce has been added in a very hot skillet or chafing dish. When cooked to desired degree of rareness, remove steaks to a hot platter. Add two jiggers of burgundy and one jigger of brandy to cooking pan; ignite and cook, shaking pan, until the fire burns out. Add the remaining sauce to the pan and blend until well integrated. Continue cooking until sauce is reduced to medium thickness. Place a mushroom cap on each steak, cover with sauce, and serve.

SCANDINAVIAN FRUIT SOUP

Makes about ten cups
1/8 pound butter
3/4 cup chopped onions
3/4 cup chopped celery and
   celery leaves
8 cups rich chicken stock
1 cup chopped dried apricots
1 cup chopped dried prunes
2 bay leaves
1/3 teaspoon dill weed
1 teaspoon granulated sugar
juice of two fat garlic cloves
1½ cups chopped unpeeled apples
1 cup half-and-half
1 cup sour cream

Danni Post, owner-chef at the Gibson House, recommends this as a prelude to duck, veal or squab. In soup pot, sauté onions and celery in melted butter until limp. Add stock, apricots, prunes and seasonings. Simmer about 45 minutes; then add apples and half-and-half. Remove a ladle of soup from the pot and whisk sour cream into it until smooth. Stir sour cream mixture into soup with a wooden spoon; add salt and pepper to taste. The apples should be slightly crisp when served. This is a basic recipe and may be varied with dried pears, peaches, green raisins or a handful of slivered almonds; but the apples and prunes should always be used.

GIBSON HOUSE SALAD DRESSING

Makes Four cups
1 cup Japanese rice vinegar
generous handful parsley
1 coarsely chopped green onion
1 walnut-size piece of fresh ginger root
1/3 cup brown sugar
1/4 teaspoon salt
1/2 teaspoon MSG
1½ cups Wesson buttery oil
1/2 cup olive oil

After much experimentation, Danni Post of the Gibson House arrived at this superb salad dressing which is good on everything except strawberries. Peel and chop ginger root. Then place all ingredients in the blender in the order in which they are listed above. Danni instructs, "Blend on high, sing a short song, and you have a frothy green salad dressing which, when refrigerated, will keep for three weeks."

SWISS FONDUE CHAMBRAISE

crushed garlic cloves
3/4 cup Chambraise strawberry aperitif
3/4 pound imported Swiss cheese
2 teaspoons cornstarch
1/2 cup cold water
salt, white pepper and nutmeg
french bread croutons

Chambraise is a French aperitif made from wild strawberries and is now on the market in America. Danni Post has created this recipe to add to her extensive fondue repertoire for special parties. To prepare the dish, rub saucepan or fondue pot thoroughly with crushed garlic cloves. Add Chambraise and bring to simmer over moderate heat. Add Swiss cheese, coarsely grated or chopped. (Danni notes that Finnish Swiss is also excellent these days.) Dissolve cornstarch in cold water and stir into the cheese mixture with a wooden spoon. Keep at simmer and stir often with a back and forth motion. Danni warns: "Never stir any fondue with a metal spoon and hard circular motion. There also is a stringy period before the ultimate blending which takes about 20 minutes. So don't panic." When blended, season to taste with salt, nutmeg and white pepper. Danni also notes that, contrary to classic opinion, Fondue can be kept warm without separating for up to 45 minutes over extremely low heat with occasional stirring. Serve fondue with croutons (bite-sized chunks of french bread, each piece having one surface of crust, toasted in the oven and served hot).

CELESTIAL PEPPER STEAK

Serves Four
2–3 pound flank steak
1 generous teaspoon whole black
   peppercorns
4 tablespoons butter
1/4 cup brandy
1/4 cup heaviest cream

Crush peppercorns very coarsely with a mortar and pestle, or roll with an empty wine bottle. (Most pepper mills grind too finely for perfection here). Pat half the crushed pepper into one side of steak. Place down on a kitchen towel and pat remaining pepper into other side. Fold towel over steak and beat with the flat side of a meat hammer or bottle until pepper is well imbedded on both sides. A few pepper usually stick to the towel. In large skillet sauté the whole steak in butter gently until desired degree of doneness. Gibson House owner-chef Danni Post recommends medium. Cut into very thin slices diagonally across the grain and remove to heated platter. Pour brandy into skillet and flame for a minute. Add cream, mix with wooden spoon and pour over sliced steak making sure any pepper in pan is included. Danni Post concludes: "Serve and be glad, for this will earn you an Arabian burp from the most well-bred guest."

LOBSTER BISQUE

Serves Eight to Ten
1½−2 pounds lobster tails
1 small carrot
1 small bay leaf
1 small onion
1 whole clove
sprig of parsley
pinch of thyme
1/3 cup dry chablis wine
5−6 tablespoons butter
1/3 cup whipping cream
1 egg yolk
5 pints clear beef broth
dash of brandy
flour

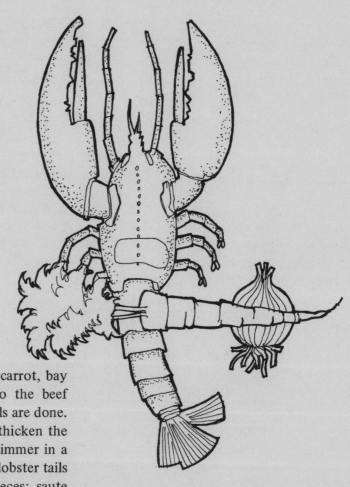

Add the lobster tails (still in their shell), carrot, bay leaf, onion, clove, parsley and thyme to the beef broth and boil slowly until the lobster tails are done. Remove lobster tails from the broth and thicken the broth with some flour and water paste; simmer in a covered pot for 90 minutes. Remove the lobster tails from their shells and cut into small pieces; saute lobster in butter and add brandy. Strain the broth and add the sauteed lobster. Beat whipping cream and egg yolks and stir slowly into the soup over low heat.

KOENIGSBERGER KLOPSE
(GERMAN MEAT BALLS)

Serves Four to Five
1 pound lean beef
1/2 pound pork
sardines
1 onion, chopped
2½ French rolls
1 large egg
salt and pepper
whipping cream
flour
1 egg yolk
fresh lemon juice
capers
bay leaf

Although the Ha'penny is basically an English restaurant, the executive chef Ralf Lindenlaub is German and will prepare German dishes for special parties. This famous recipe originated in the city of Koenigsberg. Klopse means large meatballs. To prepare the dish, soak the rolls in water; then press out all the water by squeezing the bread. Mix the bread paste with the beef, pork, sardines and onion and grind three times, finely, through a meat grinder; add salt and pepper and knead in the whole egg. Form this mixture into meat balls about two inches in diameter. In a large frying pan, bring enough salted water to cover meat balls (about four cups) and a bay leaf to a boil; add the meatballs and boil slowly until the meat is cooked throughout. Remove the meatballs onto a hot platter and keep warm. Then, over medium heat, thicken the broth in which they were cooked with a paste of flour and water; add two finely chopped sardines to the sauce. Then beat the egg yolk with about 1/2 cup of whipping cream and over low heat blend into the sauce. Finally slowly stir in lemon juice, to taste, into the sauce, and add capers to taste. The proportions of the ingredients for finishing the sauce (flour, cream and lemon juice) will vary with the amount of liquid needed to cover the meatballs, depending on the size pan used.

RUMAKI

fresh chicken livers
1 pinch anise
sliced water chestnuts (canned or fresh)
thin lean bacon
1 cup soy sauce
1 ounce grated ginger
1 teaspoon sugar
peanut oil

Mix soy sauce with ginger, sugar, and anise, and bring to a boil. Poach livers in sauce until medium done. Cut liver into oblong, finger-size cubes. Wrap raw bacon around liver with one slice of waterchestnut and secure with a tooth pick. When ready to serve, deep fry rumaki in peanut oil until bacon is crisp.

SPINACI DI CREMA SOUP

Serves Six
1 pint half-and-half
5 cups chicken broth
1 pound spinach
2 dashes worcestershire sauce
1/4 teaspoon MSG
salt
pepper

Cook spinach, drain well and chop very fine. Bring half-and-half and chicken broth to boil. Stir in rest of ingredients. Add salt and pepper to taste.

GINGER CHICKEN BAHAMIAN

Serves Two
1 2-pound fryer chicken
1/2 medium-size tomato, peeled
   and chopped
4 think slices fresh ginger root
2 ounces white wine
1 shallot clove, chopped
3 tablespoons clarified butter
3 ounces chicken broth
cornstarch

Bone, skin and quarter the chicken, leaving in the drum bones. Sauté the chicken in butter with the finely chopped shallots until golden brown. Add ginger, white wine and stock. Simmer until reduced to half. Add tomato and simmer for about 10 minutes; thicken slightly with cornstarch which has been blended with a little water. Serve with steamed rice.

PEANUT BUTTER SOUP

Makes Six Cups
2 tablespoons minced onion
3 tablespoons butter
1 tablespoon flour
1 cup peanut butter
1 quart rich chicken stock
salt and white pepper to taste
1 cup cream
Madeira wine to taste

Cook onion in butter until wilted. Whisk in flour, peanut butter and stock. Add salt and pepper and cook gently, stirring, until thickened and smooth; then add cream. Just before serving add wine to taste.

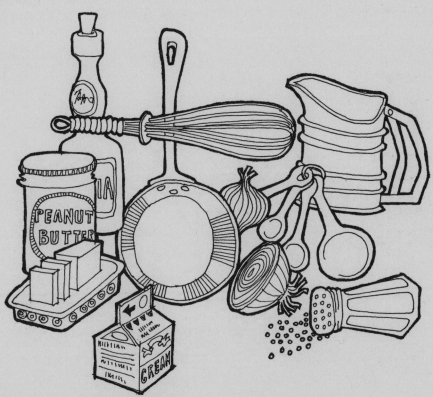

MOCHA CREAM

Ten 5-ounce glasses
4 heaping teaspoons instant coffee (Yuban)
1/2 cup boiling water
3/4 cup sugar
1 package Knox gelatine
1/2 cup cold water
1 pint whipping cream
1 teaspoon vanilla extract
toasted almonds
Creme de Cacao

The Plumed Horse is noted for owner Frances Anderson's homemade desserts. Here is one of the most popular. Dissolve coffee in boiling water and add sugar. Dissolve gelatine in cold water; melt over hot water, and combine with coffee mixture. Chill until slightly gelatinous, but not stiff. Beat with electric mixer until thick, foamy, creamy and light in color. Whip cream with vanilla and fold into mocha mixture. Chill at least four hours. To serve, pour about 1 tablespoon creme de cacao over each helping and top with toasted almonds. Or for an unusual flavor combination, serve on 1/2 canned pear.

GREEN GODDESS SOUP

Serves Eight
1 small bunch asparagus or
  10-ounce package, frozen
4 cups fresh peas or 2
  10-ounce packages, frozen
2 quarts milk
1/4 teaspoon marjoram
2 mint leaves
pinch thyme
1/2 tablespoon salt
1 large avocado
unsweetened whipped cream (garnish)
chopped parsley (garnish)

This and the following recipes from the Ranch House have been developed over the years by owner Alan Hooker, who started this restaurant with a vegetarian menu and eventually included meat dishes. Thus there is a strong emphasis on fresh vegetables and herbs (home grown at the Ranch House). To make the soup, cook the asparagus until just done in 1/4 cup water. In another pan, heat, but do not boil, the peas in 1/4 cup water. Drain peas and asparagus and liquefy by running through sieve or blender. With a pestle and mortar, grind the marjoram, mint, thyme and salt together; then heat the herb mixture in 1½ quarts of milk until warm. Next strain the peas and asparagus into the warm milk and herbs. Liquefy the avocado in 1 pint of milk and add, without straining, to the above. Heat, without boiling, and serve, garnished with whipped cream and parsley. It is extremely important not to boil or overcook the avocado or it will take on a strong acid flavor. If you are going to make the rest of the stock ahead of time, do not add the avocado until the last minute. This is one of the most popular soups at the Ranch House, and according to Alan Hooker, most people cannot identify the ingredients.

FRESH CUCUMBER SALAD DRESSING

1/2 cucumber, unpeeled
1 teaspoon salt
1 small pinch fresh ground pepper
1/4 cup vinegar
1/2 cup sour cream
dash granulated sugar

Put ingredients in blender and run for two minutes. Serve with tossed green salad.

FRENCH PEAS

For Two to Three Servings
1 10-ounce package frozen peas
   (or two cups fresh peas)
1/2 cup head lettuce, shredded
1/2 teaspoon onion salt
pinch garlic salt
pinch MSG
1/6 teaspoon ground marjoram
   (or 1/4 teaspoon marjoram leaves)
pinch sugar (optional)
2 tablespoons butter

The lettuce should be from the greenest part of the head and shredded into 1/2 inch strips. Grind seasonings together with pestle and mortar. Bring peas to boil in sufficient water to prevent sticking; add lettuce and herb mixture to nearly cooked peas and cook until just done but still firm. Add butter; toss lightly and serve immediately.

PORK TENDERLOIN MUNICH

Serves Eight
1 pork tenderloin (4–5 pounds)
butter
2 green onions, including tops, minced
1 clove garlic, minced
1/2 cup celery tops, minced
4 tablespoons flour
2 cups chicken stock
1/2 teaspoon MSG
1 teaspoon basil
2 dashes nutmeg
2 teaspoons beef extract (2 cubes)
1/4 cup dry sauterne
1/2 cup table cream
1/2 cup sour cream
grated parmesan cheese (optional)

Cut pork into thin slices that, when flattened with the side of a meat cleaver will be about two inches in diameter. Braise the pork in butter until done, very slowly at first, then with increasing heat; they must not be pink in the center. To make the sauce, melt 4 tablespoons butter in another pan; add onions, garlic, celery and sauté until the onions are soft; blend in flour; add chicken broth, MSG, basil, nutmeg, beef extract and wine; cook until thick. When thickened add cream and sour cream over very low heat and stir until well blended. To serve, spoon sauce over cooked pork and sprinkle lightly with parmesan cheese. Alan Hooker suggests shoestring potatoes, potato pancakes or noodles tossed with breadcrumbs and onion salt as accompaniments for this dish.

CALIFORNIA ORANGE-RAISIN CAKE

2 oranges
1 cup seedless raisins
1/4 pound butter
1 cup granulated sugar
2 whole eggs
1 teaspoon salt
2/3 cup buttermilk
2 cups sifted pastry flour
1 teaspoon baking soda

Sauce
3/4 cup orange juice
1/4 cup sugar
1 teaspoon curacao (optional)

Squeeze oranges and reserve juice; then grind together the orange rinds and raisins. Put ground fruit in mixing bowl and add butter, sugar, eggs, salt, buttermilk, flour and soda; beat, but not too hard. Put batter into a buttered loaf pan and bake 45 minutes to one hour at 350°. The cake is done when the dough does not stick to a toothpick inserted in the top. While the cake is baking, mix together 3/4 cup orange juice, 1/4 cup sugar and the curacao. When cake is done, spoon the sauce over it immediately, spreading evenly. Allow to cool, remove from pan and slice.

CONEY ISLAND CLAM CHOWDER

Makes ten cups
24 fresh medium-size clams, or
   1/2 pound package frozen clams
4 cups water
1 large onion, minced
1/2 stalk celery, cleaned, diced
1 green pepper, cleaned, diced
1/4 cup cooking oil
2 tablespoons flour
2 medium-size potatoes, peeled, diced
1½ cups canned stewed tomatoes, diced
salt to taste

Boil clams in water, until they open; drain, reserving liquid and shuck them. Set aside. In soup kettle heat oil; add onion, celery, and pepper; braise until transparent and tender, stirring constantly; dust with flour and stir. Add boiling clam broth, (make sure broth is hot before adding to kettle); stir until smooth and bring to soft boil. Add stewed tomatoes, with liquid, to soup. Bring to boil again; add diced potatoes; continue to simmer till potatoes are tender, (10-15 minutes). Add clams, salt to taste and bring to last boil. Serve with salt crackers.

FILLET OF SOLE MARGUERY

Serves Four
1½ pounds fillet of sole
    (about 12 medium size fillets)
salt
2 teaspoons lemon juice
1 cup sherry, plus 2 tablespoons
3 tablespoons flour
3 cups milk
2 egg yolks
3 ounces crab meat
3 ounces cooked shrimp
grated parmesan cheese
butter

Roll up fillets and place in pan. Sprinkle with salt, lemon juice, two tablespoons wine, and enough water to cover. Bring to boil. Scald milk. Melt butter and stir in flour to make light paste. Add scalded hot milk to paste, *stirring constantly*; add salt and rest of wine until smooth and starts to boil gently. Remove from heat at once and blend in egg yolks. Pour some of the cream sauce on the bottom of an ovenproof serving dish. Arrange rolled, poached fillets; surround and top with shrimp and crab meat. Pour rest of cream sauce to cover. Sprinkle generously with grated parmesan cheese and dot with butter. Place in oven and bake at 400° until golden brown.

174

San Francisco

CHICKEN ELIZABETH

Serves Four

4–5 pounds chicken, cut
  into serving pieces
salt
8 artichoke hearts, cut in half
2 slices lemon
4 tablespoons butter
6 green onions, minced
1 green pepper, minced
1/2 pound fresh mushrooms, sliced
1/2 cup sauterne
3/4 cup brown sauce (see index)

Wash and clean chicken parts; drain and rub dry with towel; sprinkle lightly with salt. Clean and wash artichoke hearts; boil with lemon slices and salt for 20 minutes or until tender; drain and set aside. (Note: you may substitute 1 package frozen artichoke hearts, cooked according to directions on the wrapper.) Heat butter in skillet and sauté chicken parts until golden brown on all sides. Add onions, green pepper and mushrooms. Continue cooking, turning occasionally so that the chicken cooks evenly and does not stick. Add wine; cover and simmer a few minutes longer. Add heated brown sauce and simmer for 15 minutes, turning chicken pieces occasionally. Add artichoke hearts and cook another 5 minutes.

It is a rare housewife, indeed, who could or would try to duplicate the basic sauce repertoire of a fine restaurant. These are made in great quantities and some, such as the basic brown sauce, take days to make. On the following pages we have presented some classic and some original recipes for making basic sauces at home with relative ease. The sauce, of course, will be better if you use home-made stock. Canned broth, or stock made from dehydrated stock base may be substituted. Sometimes, depending on the recipes, ready-made stocks can be enhanced by enrichment. In our research and testing, we have encountered a very unorthodox and easy method for enriching stocks and sauces: pureed baby foods! These are completely free of other seasonings, inexpensive, and because they are packaged in glass jars do not have a "canned" flavor. Credit for the inspiration of this idea goes to Richard Wing of the Imperial Dynasty who first suggested pureed baby food veal as a substitute for a puree of cornish game hen. We have found that, for example a little mixed chicken and vegetable baby food, can greatly enrich a chicken stock with relative ease.

HOLLANDAISE SAUCE

Makes About One Cup
2—3 egg yolks
1/4 pound butter, melted
lemon juice
salt
cayenne (optional)
paprika (optional)

A hollandaise must be made over hot water, but instead of a double boiler top, use a crock or pyrex mixing bowl that will fit in one of your saucepans, but not touch the hot water in the bottom of the pan. The heat is more evenly distributed around the sauce. Have your egg yolks at room temperature before you begin, then place them in the mixing bowl over hot water and beat them slowly with the wire whisk until they thicken. Remove from fire immediately and very slowly, a drop at a time, at first, beat in the melted butter (the sauce will not thicken if the butter is added too quickly at first). If the sauce starts to separate or curdle, beat in a tablespoon of boiling water or cream. Add seasonings and keep warm over hot, not boiling, water, until ready to serve.

BECHAMEL SAUCE (WHITE SAUCE)

Makes One Cup
2 tablespoons butter
2 tablespoons milk
1 cup milk, heated
salt and white pepper
dash nutmeg (optional)

This is the mother of all white sauces, and it is so easy to make that there is really no excuse for buying premade white sauce. Melt the butter; slowly blend in the flour to make a thick paste; then slowly pour in the milk, stirring constantly with a whisk. Add salt and pepper and stir over a very low fire for about ten minutes until the sauce is very thick.

VELOUTÉ SAUCE

Make a basic white sauce, but for half the milk substitute 1/2 cup chicken stock, or 1/2 cup veal stock, for a chicken or veal velouté; 1/2 cup clam juice for a fish velouté. To make a very rich chicken velouté, use the full cup of milk and add a teaspoon of dehydrated chicken stock base.

MORNAY SAUCE

Add one to two tablespoons each of grated Swiss and Parmesan cheese, 1 tablespoon butter and a dash of cayenne to one cup of bechamel or veloute sauce, depending on the dish with which you are serving it. For example, you may want to use a fish veloute for seafood or a chicken veloute for chicken, etc.

BROWN SAUCE: CLASSIC

The classic brown sauce or sauce espagnol is a basic ingredient in many of the recipes, particularly French, in this book. As made in the classic manner by the restaurants, a good brown sauce starts with a rich beef stock made from fresh vegetables, meat scraps and bones, simmered for hours or even days. The stock is periodically strained, reduced and enriched through a long and complicated process until it becomes sauce espangol, which has natural thickening power through the beef marrow and reduction, and natural flavor from the meats and vegetables. By further reduction, a sauce espagnol becomes a demi-glace, in which the thickening and seasoning powers are even more enhanced. Through another long process of reduction, a gelatinous paste is achieved, known as glace de viande, which, when used in tiny portions, has remarkable powers to thicken or enrich a sauce or gravy; or when diluted make a demi-glace or brown sauce. This is the way it is done in the better restaurants, and if you are truly serious about French cooking, we recommend that you make from home-made stocks and keep on hand a demi-glace or glace de viand (both of which refrigerate very well) for use as a base for your sauces. The method for this can be found in classic French cookbooks, such as Escoffier. Because few housewives will go to this trouble, we are not including the recipe here. Instead, we present a few suggestions for making a brown sauce with relative ease at home, with the warning that none will be comparable in taste to the classic sauce, which is used by better restaurants.

BROWN SAUCE OR DEMI-GLACE

Makes One to Two Cups
1½ tablespoons butter
1½ tablespoons bacon fat
2 tablespoons flour
1 carrot, sliced
1 onion, chopped
1 celery branch, chopped
3 cups beef stock
1/2 bay leaf
pinch thyme
sprig parsley
salt and pepper
garlic clove, chopped (optional)
madeira wine or red wine (optional)
worcestershire sauce (optional)
pureed veal baby food (optional)
1 tablespoon tomato paste (optional)

After much experimentation with numerous ready-made sauces or quick substitutes, we found that nothing can replace the taste of fresh vegetables, especially if you are using a canned or instant beef stock, made from a stock base, as most housewives do. Actually, except for the cooking time, this sauce is no more work than some of the substitutes suggested below, and has none of the canned or preservative flavor of the instant sauces. To make the sauce, cook the onions and celery in the melted butter and fat until lightly browned; add the flour, cooking and stirring, until the flour and butter is browned. Add remaining ingredients, except the wine and worcestershire, and simmer partially covered for 1½ to 2 hours, skimming off the fat at intervals. (To make a demi-glace, continue simmering until your liquid is reduced in half.) When sauce is cooked, strain; return to sauce pan and add salt, pepper, worcestershire and wine to taste. When finishing the sauce for a particular dish, you should keep in mind the seasonings and the subtlety of the dish. A good brown sauce has body, but the seasoning should not overpower the flavor of the final dish.

QUICK BROWN SAUCE

Makes About One Cup
2 tablespoons butter
2 tablespoons flour
1 tablespoon beef and vegetable baby food
1 tablespoon veal baby food
dash celery salt
dash onion salt
pinch thyme
1 cup beef stock
dash worcestershire sauce
sprig parsley
1/2 teaspoon Bovril (optional)
1 tablespoon madeira wine (optional)

This is my own creation and a completely unorthodox recipe which, heaven forbid, would never be found in a good restaurant kitchen. The preceeding demi-glace recipe is preferable, but if you do not have the time to simmer the sauce, this may be made when you start to prepare the dish and allowed to simmer until you are ready to use the sauce. The baby food enriches the sauce with a meat and vegetable flavor, but does not contain the strong seasonings and taste of preservative of some ready-made sauces. To make the sauce, melt butter, blend in flour and stir over low heat until the mixture is lightly browned. Add beef stock and stir until thick; then add all other ingredients except the wine and Bovril (a Canadian beef extract of great powers approaching a glace de viande). Allow to simmer until ready to use, then correct the seasoning and coloring with Bovril and wine, again keeping in mind the recipe in which you use the sauce.

INSTANT BROWN SAUCE

Makes One Cup
2 tablespoons butter
2 tablespoons flour
3/4 cup beef stock
1/4 cup V-8 Vegetable juice
dash onion salt
dash all-purpose seasoning
dash worcestershire
dash madeira or red wine
(cornstarch for optional method)

This is the least satisfactory brown sauce, but will do in an emergency. The vegetable juice adds, to a degree, the natural flavors of a good stock without leaving an overly acid flavor, such as undercooked tomato paste. There are a number of all-purpose seasonings on the market, such as Kitchen Bouquet, which will give some depth to your sauce. We have just discovered "Bisto," a French Canadian seasoning for sauces in powdered form that works very well if you need a last-minute boost to a sauce. To make, melt the butter, blend in flour and stir until golden brown. Add other ingredients and seasonings to taste. Instead of using butter and flour, you may heat the other ingredients and then thicken with cornstarch dissolved in water.

READY-MADE BROWN SAUCES

There are a number of canned and dehydrated brown gravies on the market which may be substituted for brown sauce, with varying results. We recommend the dehydrated to eliminate the danger of a "canned" flavor penetrating your sauce. Some of these are highly seasoned, so be careful that the seasoning does not overpower your dish; for example buy the plain brown gravy, not onion gravy, etc. In some gourmet food stores, it is possible to buy a fresh glace de viande, which simply needs to be diluted to make a brown sauce, and will keep refrigerated for weeks. If you can find this, it is probably the best solution. S. S. Pierce produces a canned bordelaise sauce, which can also be substituted for brown sauce.

MUSHROOM SAUCE

butter
1/4 to 1/2 pound mushrooms, minced
2 tablespoons shallots or onions, minced
1/2 cup dry wine
1 cup brown sauce
chopped parsley
pinch basil or tarragon
cream (optional)

For the ultimate in mushroom flavor, squeeze your mushrooms until they are free of all liquid before adding them to the sauce. Melt several tablespoons butter in a skillet and sauté the mushrooms and shallots until tender. Add wine (red, white or sherry depending upon the delicacy of the dish you will serve with the sauce) and cook until the wine is almost cooked away. Add other ingredients, except cream, and simmer for about five minutes. Correct seasoning with salt and pepper; remove from fire and finish sauce with 4 to 8 tablespoons of softened butter and a little heavy cream. The seasonings for this recipe depend upon the accompanying dish. An easier version may be made, by mixing 2 tablespoons of flour into the mushrooms and onions after they are cooked and substituting 1 cup beef or chicken stock (again depending on the dish) for the brown sauce.

DESSERT CREPES

To Make Eight Pancakes
3 whole eggs
2 tablespoons flour, sifted
1 tablespoon water
1 tablespoon milk
pinch of salt
dash of orange water
butter

Add water, salt and orange water to lightly beaten eggs; then blend this mixture into the sifted flour. Whip batter while adding the milk until the mixture is the consistency of oil. (A drop of orange liquer or orange juice may be substituted for the orange water.) Chill batter for several hours. In a 5-inch round skillet melt just enough butter to cover the bottom of the skillet and, when melted, brush out excess butter. If you have never made crepes before you will probably have to experiment with several on timing and temperature until you get the knack. But don't be discouraged if the first few are not exactly up to Le Trianon standards; the technique is usually mastered quickly and from then on it's easy. When the pan is moderately hot, remove from fire and pour about 1½ tablespoons batter into the center of the pan, while quickly jiggling the pan with your right hand so the batter evenly covers the bottom of the pan. Return to heat and cook until lightly browned (about a minute). Then bang the pan on the side of your range to loosen the crepe; loosen edges with a spatula; and gently turn or flip. Cook the other side; remove from pan and repeat the process until you have used all your batter. These may be made ahead of time.

ENTREE CRÊPES

Makes 12 Six-Inch Crêpes
1 cup water
1 cup milk
4 eggs
salt
2 cups flour, sifted
4 tablespoons butter, melted

These are slightly heavier and thicker than the dessert crêpe above, and this batter should be used with meat, poultry and seafood fillings. The method is the same as for the dessert crêpes, except that you should use more batter for each pancake.

APPETIZERS

Cheese Burek, Adriatic, 78
Chinese Raviolis (Chiao Tzu), Mandarin, 27
Coo-Coo Clams, Lupo's, 42
Cornish Pasties, The Coachman, 149
Escargots, Imperial Dynasty, 104
Frog Leg Crepes with Curry Sauce, Imperial Dynasty, 100
Guacamole, Los Gallos, 14
La Croquette de Crevette, Old Brussels, 128
Lamb Tartare (Chee Kufta), Haji Baba, 76
Meat Burek, Adriatic, 79
Oysters au Champagne, Le Trianon, 122
Piroshki, Bull Valley Inn, 62
Rumaki, King's Four in Hand, 164
Scampi and Prosciutto, Matteo's, 40
Scampi, Ruggero's, 47
Steamed Clams Mariniere, Olive Mill Bistro, 130
Stuffed Mushrooms, Imperial Dynasty, 104
Swiss Fondue Chambraise, Gibson House, 160
Tartare Steak, Riviera, 137

SOUPS

Anthony's Cioppino, 34
Black Cherry Soup, The Tower, 140
Bouillabaisse, Place Pigalle, 134
Caraway Seed Soup, Manka's, 65
Chief Heinz' Lentil Soup, Rolf's, 68
Cock-A-Leekie Soup, The Coachman, 148
Coney Island Clam Chowder, Sam's Grill, 173
Consomme Belle Vue, Le Petit Chateau, 118
Cream of Abalone Soup, Gallatin's, 156
Cream of Watercress Soup, Riviera, 136
Cucumber and Yogurt Soup, L'Odeon, 81
Gazpacho, Matador, 8
Greek Lemon Soup, The Clock, 146
Green Goddess Soup, The Ranch House, 169
Hot and Sour Soup, Mandarin, 26
Lazyman's Cioppino, Scoma's, 52
Lobster Bisque, Ha'Penny, 162

Oyster Soup, The Brambles, 145
Peanut Butter Soup, Edith Palmer's Country Inn, 167
Scandinavian Fruit Soup, Gibson House, 158
Spinaci Di Crema Soup, King's Four In Hand, 165
Spinach and Leek Soup, Chez Gerard, 92
Split Pea Soup, Discovery Inn, 152
Stratacelli alla Romano, Orsi's, 44

CHEESE, EGGS, AND PASTA

Cannelloni, Doro's, 36-7
Cheese Burek, Adriatic, 78
Fettuccine alla Romana, Raffaello, 50
Quiche Lorraine, L'Orangèrie, 126
Spaghetti alla Carbonara, Vanessi's, 56
Swiss Fondue Chambraise, Gibson House, 160

SALADS AND SALAD DRESSINGS

Basic Salad Dressing, Charles, 86
Bibb Lettuce Vinagrette, Kirkeby's, 106
Chef Heinz' Roquefort Dressing, Rolf's, 69
Chile Salad, El Poche Cafe, 13
Cucumber Salad (Sunomono), Yamato, 29
Fresh Cucumber Salad Dressing, The Ranch House, 170
Gibson House Salad Dressing, 159
Guacamole Salad, Los Gallos, 14
Salad Exotique, L'Auberge, 112
Spinach Salad Flambe, Chez Cary, 89
Tomato and Mushroom Salad, Charles', 86

BEEF

Beef Risotto, Discovery Inn, 154
Beef Stroganoff, Discovery Inn, 153
Boeuf Bourguignon, Chez Marguerite, 96
Braised Oxtails Jardiniere, Place Pigalle, 135
Butter-Yaki, Yamato, 30
Carbonade Flamande, Old Brussels, 129
Carne Asada, Los Gallos, 15

Steamed Clams Mariniere, Olive Mill Bistro, 130
Steamed Whole Fish A La Lee On, Madame Wu's, 21
Tetsu-yaki, Yamato, 31
White Fish (Brodetto), Tana's, 54

VEAL

Escalope de Ternera, Matador, 11
Grenadin de Veau Grand Dufour, Le Trianon, 121
Mignon de Veau, La Bourgogne, 116
Miro's Special, Old Trieste, 43
Veal Cordon Bleu, Riviera, 138
Veal Cutlet, Vanessi's, 57
Veal Kidneys, Flamed, L'Auberge, 113
Veal Matteo, 41
Veal Paolo, Doro's, 39
Veal Paprikash, Manka's, 66
Veal Picatta, Ruggero's, 48
Scalopines de Veau aux Cepes, The Tower, 141
Sweetbreads a la Serge, Ondine's, 132

VEGETABLES

Epinards a la Chef Heinz, Rolf's, 70
French Peas, The Ranch House, 170
Garden Orientale a la Lee On, Madame Wu's, 20
Potato Pancakes, Schroeder's, 73
Rice Pilaf, L'Odeon, 82
Red Cabbage, German Style, Schroeder's, 71
Stuffed Mushrooms, Imperial Dynasty, 103
Tomatoes Medici, Doro's, 38
Zucchini and Rice au Bouillon, L'Auberge, 114

DESSERTS

Banana Virginia, Chez Cary, 91
California Orange-Raisin Cake, The Ranch House, 172
Cassata, Bull Valley Inn, 64
Cherries Jubilee, Kirkeby's, 109
Crepes Aegean, L'Odeon, 83
Crepes Suzette, Le Trianon, 124
Fruit Trifle, The Coachman, 151

Lemon Tort, Manka's, 67
Mocha Cream, Plumed Horse, 168
Omelette Norvegienne, L'Escoffier, 124
Orange Petit Chateau Flambe, 120
Peach Flambe, L'Auberge, 111
Souffle Grand Marnier, La Bourgogne, 117.
Strawberries Ruggero, 49
Zabaione, Raffaello's, 51
Zuppa Inglese, Orsi's, 46

SAUCES

Bearnaise Sauce, Charles, 87
Bechamel Sauce, 179
Brown Sauce, 180 to 184
Catherine Ghio's Tomato Sauce, 35
Clam and Wine Sauce, Chez Marguerite, 95
Cucumber Soubise Sauce, Imperial Dynasty, 102
Curry Sauce, Chez Gerard, 90
Curry Sauce A La Richard Wing, Imperial Dynasty, 101
Demi-Glace Sauce, 181
Duxelle of Mushrooms, L'Auberge, 113
Hollandaise Sauce, 178
Madeira Sauce, Riviera, 138
Marinara Sauce, Doro's, 37
Marinara Sauce, Matteo's, 41
Mornay Sauce, 179
Mushroom Sauce, 185
Salsa a la Los Gallos, 15
Supreme Sauce, Old Trieste, 43
Tomato Sauce, Scoma's, 52
Veloute Sauce, 179
Watercress Sour Cream Sauce
  (For Fish), Le Petit Chateau, 119

BREADS, ROLLS, AND BATTERS

Crepes, Dessert, 186
Crepes, Entree, 187
Jinny Smedsrud's Famous Oatmeal Bread, Bonanza Inn, 144
Marjorie Dehr's Rolls, Discovery Inn, 155

OTHER BOOKS FROM 101 PRODUCTIONS

Cooking with Herbs, by Alan Hooker
Soup, by Coralie Castle
Vegetarian Gourmet Cookery, by Alan Hooker
Greek Cooking for the Gods, by Eva Zane
Mammy Pleasant's Cookbook, by Helen Holdredge
Pots and Pans, Etc., by Gertrude Harris
Ecology at Home, by Jacqueline Killeen
Festivals in California, by Christine Austin
101 Nights in California, a guide to restaurants
Hard Times Cookbook, by Gloria Vollmayer
and Carmen Wyllie